CUNEIFORM TEXTS

IN THE

METROPOLITAN MUSEUM OF ART

EDITED AND TRANSLATED

BY

ALFRED B. MOLDENKE, PH. D.

ISBN: 978-1-63182-834-8

Printed: March 2023

Published and Distributed By:
Lushena Books
607 Country Club Drive, Unit E
Bensenville, IL 60106
www.lushenabks.com

ISBN: 978-1-63182-834-8

PREFACE TO PARTS I. & II.

In undertaking the publication of the cuneiform texts in the Metropolitan Museum of Art of New York City, I was prompted by the desire to render this small but interesting treasure accessible to students of the Semitic languages.

These two parts are the first of a series of seven parts to be published as quickly as time permits. The texts referred to, are divided into two collections, known as the "*Egibi*," and the "*Ward*" collections. The former was purchased in 1878 from the British Museum, and the latter from the Rev. Dr. W. H. Ward of the Wolfe Expedition, by Gen. C. P. di Cesnola, the Director of the Museum. Part I contains 21 texts of the *Egibi*, and Part II, 35 of the *Ward* collection.

Part I was published by me in June of this year under the title *Babylonian Contract Tablets in the Metropolitan Museum of Art*. The causes that led me to republish it here were numerous and weighty. Chief among them I may mention that the volume was published as a doctor's dissertation, and in the hurry to get the book into print, many typographical errors were overlooked, and mistakes that should have been corrected, were left untouched. I trust that in the present volume all such errors will have been avoided. Another cause was the desire of the Museum authorities to have some publication of their collections to offer to inquiring strangers and to the learned public. I regret that time did not permit me to have the Babylonian equivalents of many of the Assyrian signs cast. With the type at my disposal, however, the cuneiform text has been made to appear as similar as possible to the original writing on the contract tablets. Also in the transliteration many peculiarities will be found, which I have seen fit to discard in succeeding parts. Part I must, in fact, be considered a book by itself, complete and independent of any other part. The indices of Part I have also been incorporated in the preface instead of being placed at the end as in the first edition. The correspondence of such letter as *ḫ*, *š*, *ḳ*, etc., to Hebrew letters will be readily seen.

Part II will be found to be, I trust, an improvement upon Part I. Not only is the type of the cuneiform text exactly similar (excepting peculiarities of hand-writing of the individual scribes) to the original characters on the contract tablets, but the distinction between the transliteration and the translation is brought out more clearly by the use of Italic type for the former instead of Antique Roman. The notes have also been made as short as possible, and they confine themselves to explanations of the text and to references. They have been relegated to the end.

The remaining texts in the Metropolitan Museum of Art have been divided for publication as follows:

Part III will contain Nos. 1-10 of the *Egibi*, and Nos. 16-45 of the *Ward* collection, Total: 40 Texts of the reigns of Nebuchadnezzar, Amelu-Marduk and Nergalsharusur.

Part IV will contain Nos. 32-36 of the *Egibi* and Nos. 66-77 of the *Ward* collection. Total: 17 texts of the reigns of Cyrus and Cambyses.

Part V will contain Nos. 37-56 of the *Egibi*, and Nos. 78-120 of the *Ward* collection. Total: 51 texts, chiefly of Darius.

Part VI will contain about 50 undated contract tablets, 5 belonging to the *Egibi* collection.

Part VII will contain all the Assyrian, Babylonian and Accadian texts of the *Ward* collection not included in any of the other parts.

In conclusion I wish to express my most sincere thanks to the Museum authorities, especially to Gen. C. P. di Cesnola and to Prof. I. H. Hall, for their kind and liberal treatment and for the manifold facilities that they have courteously placed at my disposal. Also to my brother, the Rev. Dr. C. E. Moldenke, who is at present publishing a catalogue of the Museum's magnificent collection of Egyptian antiquities, I wish to express my thanks for his kind help, especially in the drawing and procuring of the signs that are so frequently used in Part II, and will be required for the publication of the remaining parts.

NEW YORK CITY,
Oct. 1st, 1893.

A. B. MOLDENKE.

PART I.

LIST OF BOOKS QUOTED, AND ABBREVIATIONS.

Abel und Winckler, Keilschrifttexte zum Gebrauch bei Vorlesungen. (Sanherib, Asarhaddon) Berlin 1890.

Beiträge zur Assyriologie und Vergleichenden Semitischen Sprachwissenschaft, herausgegeben von Fr. Delitzsch und P. Haupt. Leipzig 1889 - 1892. . . *B. A.*

Brünnow, R. E., A Classified List &c. Leyden 1889.

Delitzsch, Fr., Assyrische Grammatik. Berlin 1889.

" Assyrische Lesestücke. Dritte Auflage. (Sintflutbericht) Leipzig 1885.

" Assyrische Studien. Heft I. Leipzig 1874.

Babylonian and Oriental Record. London. . . . . . . *BOR*

Hoffmann, Auszüge aus syrischen Acten persischer Märtyrer. Leipzig 1880.

Hommel, F., Geschichte Babyloniens und Assyriens. Berlin 1885 - 1889.

Jensen, P., Die Kosmologie der Babylonier. Strassburg 1890.

Lagarde, P., Agathangelus. (Abhandlungen der Königlichen Gesellschaft der Wissenschaften zu Göttingen, Vol. XXXV) 1887.

Lotz, W., Die Prisma-Inschrift des assyr. Königs Tiglathpileser I. Leipzig 1880. . *LTP*

Peiser, F. E., Babylonische Verträge des Berliner Museums. Berlin 1890. . *Bab. Ver.*

" Keilschriftliche Actenstücke. Berlin 1889.

Pognon, H., L'inscription de Bavian. Paris 1879.

Sayce, A. H., Lectures on the Origin and Growth of Religion (Hibberd Lectures). London 1877.

Schroeder, Phönicische Sprache mit Entwurf einer Grammatik. Halle 1869.

Sitzungsbericht der Königlichen Akademie der Wissenschaften zu Berlin. 1889.

Smith, P., Thesaurus Syriacus. Clarendon Press, Oxon. 1879.

Smith, S. A., Keilschrifttexte Asurbanipals. Leipzig 1887 - 1889.

Strassmaier, J. N., Babylonische Texte, Heft I - VII. Inschriften von Nabonidus, Nabuchodonosor und Cyrus, von den Thontafeln des Britischen Museums copiert &c. Leipzig 1887 - 1890. . . . *Strass. Nabn., Nbk., Cyr.*

Strassmaier, J. N., Inschriften im Museum zu Liverpool. Leyden 1885.

" Verhandlungen des 5ten Internationalen Orientalisten Congresses zu Berlin. 1881.

Tallqvist, K. L., Die Sprache der Contracte Nabû-nâ'ids. Helsingfors 1890. . *Tallq.*

Tiele, C. P., Babylonisch-assyrische Geschichte. Gotha 1886 - 1888.

Zeitschrift für Assyriologie. Leipzig 1883 - 1892. . . . . . *Z. A.*

Zeitschrift der Deutschen Morgenländischen Gesellschaft. . . . *ZDMG*

INDEX OF PROPER NAMES.

The superior numerals refer to the lines of the tablets, while the other numerals refer to the tablets.

I. CITIES.

(din)Babilu 11$^{19, 21}$ 12$^{21, 22}$ 13$^{17, 19}$ 14^{25} 15$^{14, 16}$ 16^{17} 17^{14} 18^{12} [19^{11}] 20^{15} 21$^{20, 22}$ 22$^{16, 17}$ 23$^{12, 14}$ 24^{16} 25$^{18, 20}$ 26$^{22, 24}$ 27$^{13, 14}$ 28$^{16, 17}$ 29^{30} 30$^{15, 17}$ 31^{13}

Babilu 14^{27} 16^{19} 17$^{5, 16}$ 20^{13} 24^{14} 29^{26}

Barsiba 18^{11}

alû Bit-šar-i 31^{11}

alû Kas-sur (?) 13^{5}

II. MONTHS.

Nisannu 26^{23} 28^{15} 29^{28}

Airu 22^{4} 14^{25}

Simanu 30^{15}

Dûzu 25^{18} 31^{12}

Ululu 27^{12} 17$^{4, 14}$

Tašritu 13^{17}

Samna 27$^{4, 5}$ 15^{15}

Samna-am-a 21^{20}

Šabaṭu 19^{9} 20$^{5, 14}$ 23^{13} 24^{14}

Adaru 11^{19} 12^{21} 16^{17} 18^{11} 22^{16} 23^{6}

III. GODS.

Bil 21^{19} 25^{16}

Gu-la 24^{12}

Za-ri-ḳu 17^{12} 25^{13}

Na-na 17^{16} 30$^{5, 6}$

Ninip 16$^{4, 17}$

Ša-maš 18^{9}

IV. PERSONS.

Ai 11^{4} 22^{12}

ilu **Î-a-na-ṣir** 25^{6}

ilu **A-ba-ba-ti-la** 27^{3}

Ab-la-a 30^{11}

Ab-la-da 18^{5}

Ib-na-a 21^{16}

Î-gi-bi 12^{8} 14^{18} 20$^{4, 18}$ 21$^{7, 12}$ 22^{3} 23^{6} 28^{6} 29^{3} 31$^{2, 3}$ 26$^{3, 20}$

Idanin-Nabû 18^{10}

Id-da-a 25^{3}

Iddin-........ 21^{1}

Iddin-Bil 23^{9}

Iddin-Marduk 17$^{1, 3}$ 18^{1} 23^{10} 24^{1} 25^{3} 28^{10} 19^{3}

Ia-ḫa-ta 21^{3}

Iddin-Nabû 20^{11} 20^{25} 31^{6}

Iddin-na-ḫu-nun-ṭi-iš-Marduk 28^{13}

Iddin-na-Nabû 21^{15}

Aḫa-ba-ni 17^{14} 25^{16}

Iṭir-Marduk 22^{13}

Iṭir-ša-na-nim 12^{5}

U-ka-ga-tu-ra-šad 30[7]
ilu Îllatu-u 11[9] 14[25]
Î-mid-su 19[9]
Amtu 28[2]
Î-sag-gil-ai 26[8]
A-pak-kal-ia 26[20]
Îpi-iš-ilu 13[2] 14[19] 22[14] 30[11]
Iķbi-[Marduk] 29[6]
Iķiša-apla 26[19]
Iķi-ša-apla 17[2] 18[3] 23[9] 24[3 8] 25[4] 28[11] 31[6]
A-ra-bi 17[3]
Ir-ba-Marduk 14[24]
Ardi-ia 29[24]
Arad-Bil 13[14 15] 22[15] 29[6]
Arad-Marduk 21[18] 22[3] 25[9 17]
Arad-Nirgal 22[12] 25[15]
A-ša-a-na-šad 25[8]
It-ik-kal-a 15[3]
It-ti-.......... 25[21]
Itti-.......... 20[24]
Itti-Marduk-......-balaṭu 26[1]
Itti-Marduk-balaṭu 26[1] 27[1]
Itti-Nabû-balaṭu 29[26] 31[10]

Ba-bu-tu 12[20] 26[4 21]
Babu-u-tu 27[11]
Ba-la-ṭu 11[1] 26[19]
Bil-.......... 15[8]
Bil-uballi-iṭ 15[12 13]
Bil-ibni 31[9]
Bil-iddin 13[3 6 10 11] 14[7] 29[4 7 20]
Bil-di-ḫir 20[23]
Bil-idanin 28[12]
Bil-zir-ibni 26[16]
Bil-aḫi-iddin 27[12]
Bil-aḫi-iķi-ša 19[6]
Bil-ḫarran 17[9]
Bil-iṭir 27[9]
Bil-i-ṭir 31[11]
Bil-i-ṭi-ru 11[4] 29[27]
Bil-kaṣir 12[19]
Bil-Marduk 27[8]
Bil-naṣir 25[22]
Bil-apal-iddin 11[12] 19[8] 24[9 12]
Bil-pat-ta-nu 12[17]
Bil-iķi-ša 16[12] 30[2 5]
Bil-ri-man-ni 12[20] 24[5]
Bil-šum-iškun 23[10]
Bil-šu-nu 12[17] 19[7] 30[5]
Bani-ia 29[14]
Bani-i-a 11[8] 29[4 7]
Bâni-um-ma-gu 27[12]
Ba-ni-ia 12[3] 15[9] 16[3 18] 20[11](?)
Bani-a-tu-i-sag-ila 16[1 10]
Bit-ti-ia 21[19] 25[17]

Gu-la-ri-nin-ni 11[2] 12[1 10 13]

Da-bi-ia 13[16]
Da-bi-bi 21[17]
Du-ub-bi 20[11]
Du-um-muķ 13[15]
Dan-a 11[14]
Di-na-a 30[12]
ilu Dainu-zir-ibni 30[16]

Zir-ai 21[16]
Zi-ri-ia 15[11] 27[8]
Zir-ukin 24[11]
Zir-ûtu 22[14]

Ḫa-an-na-'-šu 16[9]
Ḫu-nu-ti-tiš-Šamaš-balaṭu 11[3]
Ḫu-pu-u 28[4]

Ka-di-di 14[22]
Ka-di-nu 12[18]

Bil-aḫi-iḳi-ša	apal-šu ša	Bil-šu-nu	apal		19 [6]
Bil-ḫarran	" "	Mu-šal-lim-mu	"	amilu šangu Nana	17 [9]
Bil-iṭir	" "	Nabû-šum-uṣur	"	Rammân-šum-uṣur	27 [2]
Bil-kaṣir *Scribe of the 12th Tablet.*	" "	Bil-ri-man-ni	"	Ba-bu-tu	12 [19]
Bil-apal-iddin	" "	Î-mid-su			19 [8]
Bil-apal-iddin *Scribe of the 24th Tablet.*	" "	Daḫ-ḫi-ša(?)	"	Nabû-lit-su	24 [12]
Bil-apal-iddin	" "	Nabû-[iddin?]	"	Rammân-šum-iddin	24 [9]
Bil-apal-iddin	" "	Nabû-aḫi-irba	"	Ḳur-ban	11 [12]
Bil-ri-man-ni	" "	Marduk-mušallim			24 [5]
Bil-šu-nu	" "	Bil-iḳi-ša	"	amilu šangu Nana	30 [5]
Bil-.........	" "	Nabû-šum-uṣur	"	Bani-[ia]	15 [8]
Ba-ni-ia *Scribe of the 16th Tablet*	" "	Nabû-šum-iddin	"	amilu šangu Ninip	16 [3, 16]
Bâni-um-ma-gu *Scribe of the 27th Tablet*	" "	Bil-aḫi-iddin-na	"	Ṣir-diš-bit	27 [12]
Dainu-zir-ibni	" "	Ab-la-a	"	Îpi-iš-ilu	30 [10]
Zir-ûtu	" "	Nabû-zir-iddin			22 [14]
Ḫu-nu -ti-tiš-Šamaš-balaṭu	" "	Ai	"	Bil-i-ṭi-ru	11 [3]
Ki-di-nu	" "	Marduk-iṭi-ir	"	Rammân-u-mi-i	12 [10]
Kal-ba-a	" "	Ia-ḫa-ta			21 [2, 9]
		Nabû-aḫi-iddin	"	Î-gi-bi	31 [2, 4, 6]
La-a-ba-ši	" "	Zi-ri-ia	"	Na-ba-ai	27 [3]
La-di-pi	" "	Di-na-a			30 [12]
Lu-uṣ-a-na-nûri-Marduk	" "	Ki-rib-ti	"	Î-gi-bi	21 [11]
Marduk-iddin	" "	Marduk-ipi-iš	"	Zir-ai	21 [13]
Marduk-zir-ibni	" "	Šu-la-a	"	Naṣir-ḫat-ai	14 [22]
Marduk-iṭi-ir	" "	Ri-mut	"	Arad-Nirgal	25 [14]
Marduk-mušallim *Scribe of the 17th Tablet*	" "	Nabû-šip-uṣur	"	Aḫa-ba-ni	17 [14]
Marduk-iḳi-ša-an-ni	" "	Bani-i-a	"	Îllatu-u	11 [8]
*Marduk-iḳi-ša-an-ni	" "	Ba-ni-ia	"	....-uṣur-bilu-u	12 [2, 14]
Marduk-šarrâ-ni	" "	Bil-iḳi-ša	"	Ša-ṭâbti-šu	16 [11]
Nabû-balaṭ-iddin	" "	Ṣil-la-a	"	Na-ši-ir-na-a	20 [1]
Nabû-balaṭ-su-iḳbi	" "	Bani-ia	"	Ri-šar-tum	29 [13]
Nabû-balaṭ-su-[iḳbi]	" "	Zir-ia	"	amilu bânû	15 [10]
Nabû-ban-aḫa	" "	Iḳi-ša-apla	"	Na-din-Marduk	24 [3]
Nabû-ga-mil	" "	Nabû-mu-ši-ni-ud-da	"	Î-sag-gil-ai	26 [17]

* Very likely identical with the preceding. The family name is broken off at the beginning, hence the latter is uncertain.

Šu-la-a	apal-šu ša	**Iḳi-ša-apla**	apal	**Iddin-Bil**	**23** [8]
Šapik-zir	" "	**Nabû-šum-iddin**	"	**Na-din-ši-bar**	**15** [1 6]
Šapik-zir	" "	**Nirgal-musallim**	"	**Sin-ga-ga-nim-mi**	**16** [14]
Ša-aš-Bil-ṭi	" "	**Nabû-itti-apli**	"	**Ḫu-pu-u**	**28** [8]
Tab-ni-i / **Tab-ni-i-a** / **Tabni-i-a** amilu šangu ilu Zariḳu	" "	**Nabû-aḫi-iddin**		amilu šangu ilu **Zariḳu**	**17** [11]
				amilu šangu ilu **Šamaš**	**18** [7]
					25 [12]
Tab-ni-i-a *Scribe of the 11 th Tablet.*	" "	**Nabû-mu-u-da**	"	**Nu-u-pu**	**11** [17]
......**-šum-ukin**	" "	**Iddin-**......			**21** [1]
....	" . "	**Id-da-a**			**25** [1]

The following five names are those of the women whose genealogy is given in these texts. They are appended here, because the persons can thus be more readily found in other texts.

Amtu	marat-su ša	**Marduk-šum-uṣur**			**28** [3]
Bani-a-tu-i-sag-ila	" "	**Nabû-šum-iddin**			**16** [1 10]
Nabû-u-šu-da-ḳâtâ	" "	**Ta-k iš-Gu-la**	apal	amilu **ḳipu**	**22** [5]
Nu-ub-ta-a	" "	**Nabû-mu-ši-ni-ud-da**	"	**Î-sag-gil-ai**	**26** [4]
Ni-lat-tum	" "	**Arad-Bil**		**Iḳbi-[Marduk?]**	**29** [6]

A GLOSSARY

OF THE ASSYRIAN WORDS OCCURRING IN THE TEXTS.

u *and*. Very frequent.

[amilu]**IB-bani** *carpenter*. 21[13]

abâlu *to bring*. **iṭ-bal** 29[14]

adi *together with*. **a-di** 14[1] 16[7] 18[3] 28[9] **a-di-i** 29[11] **a-di ili** *until*. 22[7] 29[13] **a-di ili ša** *until that*. 26[14]

idu *hand, side*. **i-di** 26[10]

aḫu *portion, half*. **a-ḫi** 13[6] 15[5] **a-ḫa-a-ta-šu-nu** 25[18] **it-ti a-ḫa-miš** *with one another*. 28[9]

itiru *to receive*. **iṭ-ṭi-ru** 17[4] **i-ṭi-ru** 22[10] 24[7] **i-tir-tum** 28[3] **i-ṭi-ru** *pay*. 28[1]

akâlu *to eat, consume*. **ik-kal** 13[7] 15[6]

ul *not*. 13[8] 28[9] 29[17 18]

ilu *god*. Determinative. Frequent.

alû *city*. 13[5] 31[11] **ina ali u ṣiri** *in city and country*. 15[4]

ili *about*. 31[4] For other instances see under **adi**, **ultu**, **ana**, and **ina**.

ilu *to go up, make out*. **il-li** 13[9] **il-la-'** 12[14] **i-'-i-li** 12[6] **i-ti-li** 25[4 7] **ul-ti-la** 31[5]

alâdu *to bring forth*. **tu-li-da** 11[6]

alâku *to go*. **il-lak** (in the phrase **našutti illak**) *possesses*. 13[11] **il-la-ku** ibid. 14[9]

alpu *cattle*. **al-pa** 20[5]

i-lat *to be additional*. 13[11] 30[8]

ultu *from*. 15[7] 21[4] **ul-tu ili** *below*. 13[7] **ultu ili mi-ḫir-tu** *in behalf of*. 18[4]

umû *day*. 11[19] 12[21] 13[18] 14[26] 15[14] 16[18] 17[6 15] 18[11] 19[10] 20[5 14] 21[21] 22[16] 23[13] 24[14] 25[19] 26[23] 27[13] 28[15] 29[28] 30[16] 31[13]

amilu *man*. Determinative. Frequent.

amilûtu *slave*. **a-mi-lut-tum** 20[3]

ummu *mother*. 26[26] **ummi-šu** 29[20]

[amilu]**I.MAŠ** *priest*. 21[19]

a.an Added to numerals.

ânu *not to be*. **ia-a-nu** 13[12]

ana a-na *to*. 11[5] 12[6 11] 15[7] 20[7] 21[6] 28[3] 29[9] 31[4 8] *for*. 11[7] 12[3 4 10] 15[3] 17[7] 21[8] 25[22] 29[5 16 17] *as regards*. 13[4] *to the value of*. 14[3 6 10 14 15] **a-na ili** *against*. 13[9] *on account*. 25[4 7]

ina *in, at, for, after*. 12[7] 13[5 6] 14[3] 15[4 5 6] 17[4] 18[6 7] 19[5] 21[3] 22[4] 24[5] 26[20] 27[4 5] 30[9] **ina ili** *against, to be received of*. 13[3] 14[6 7] 15[3 4] 16[3] 17[3] 20[3] 22[3] 23[4] 24[3 4] 26[3] 27[3 6] **ina ili-šu** 17[8] 27[7] **ina ili-šu-nu** 26[8] **ina lib-bi** *thereupon*. 26[6] **ina ḳâtâ** *from, from the hands of*. 12[4] 18[3] 19[3] 28[5] 29[4] 30[6]

an-us-ti-nu 25[9]

u.an.tim *receipt*. 12[6 12] 14[7] 28[6] 31[1]

aplu *son*. construct: **apal**. Very frequent.

ipišu *to receive, acquire*. **i-pu-šu** 29[5] 31[3] **i-pu-šu** 12[5] **ip-pu-uš** 15[4] **ip-pu-uš-šu** 13[5] **i-pu-uš-ša** 28[7] **i-piš-ša** 31[1]

iṣu *wood*. Also determinative. [iṣu]**iṣu** 14[15]

arad šarrûtu An official. 11[18]

irṣitu *land*. Determ. following **Babilu** (not transliterated in this book). Also 31[11]

[amilu]**IR.ŠAL.TAB(?).ŠA** 23[12]

išu *to be*. **i-ša** 23[16] **i-šu-[u]** 26[14]

aššâbu *to sit down*. **u-šib-u** *placed*. 26[9] **a-ša-bi** *presence*. 26[25]

aššatu *wife*. **aššati-šu** 16[5] **aššat-su** 18[5] **aššat-šu** 26[4] *servant*. **aš-šat-ti** 16[6] **aš-šat-su-nu** 16[9]

ištin *one*. **išti-in** 31[7]

ia-[a-tu(?)] *I*. 26[12]

itti *with*. **it-ti** 13[6] 28[9] **it-ti-i** 15[5]

itiḳu *to take away*. **i-ti-iḳ** 13[6 9]

utru *profit*. **u-tur** 13[6] 15[6]

balâṭu *to live*. **bal-tu-u** 28[9]

[amilu]**bânû** *carpenter*. 15[11]

bašû *to be*. **ba-ši-i** 18[12]

bîtu *house.* 26 [10] bît-ia 26 [10] bît-su-nu 26 [12]

gabbu *all.* gab-bi 26 [13] gab-bu-tu 16 [6]

gabrû *rival, another, duplicate.* gab-ri 12 [12]

gallu *male slave.* gal-la 25 [11] gal-la gal-la 14 [16] amilu gal-la 17 [3]

gallatu *female slave.* gal-lat-su 22 [6] amilu gal-lat-su 11 [3]

amilu GIM is to be read amilu bânû *carpenter.*

gamru *entire, all.* gam-ru-tu 12 [4] gam-ru-tum *fullness.* 11 [7]

gimru *vegetables.* gim-ru 30 [9]

ginû *offering, sacrifice.* gi-nu-u 28 [7] amilu ni-ṣur-gi-na 28 [12, 14] (see note.)

gu-ri-nu *threshed* (?) 14 [13]

gurru A measure for dry and liquid substances. gur 25 [20]

giśimmaru *datepalm.* 28 [7]

DU See manzazu.

dibbu *complaint, lawsuit.* dib-bi 14 [3]

daḫ-ḫu-tum *additional, further demand.* 18 [13]

amilu daînu *judge.* 23 [5] daini 16 [13]

dannu *large.* karpatu dan-nu-tu *jar, vessel.* 14 [1] dan-nu 14 [3]

duppu *contract tablet.* 28 [7] 31 [1]

dupsaru *scribe.* dupsar 12 [14] dup-sar 23 [11] amilu dupsar 11 [17] 12 [19] 13 [18] 14 [24] 15 [13] 16 [16] 17 [13] 20 [12] 21 [18] 22 [15] 24 [13] 25 [17] 26 [21] 27 [13] 28 [13] 29 [26] 30 [13] 31 [10]

sir-mu-u An iron instrument. 14 [13]

sittu *portion, share.* 15 [5]

ḫubullu *interest.* 19 [1] 24 [5] ḫubulla-śu 22 [5] ina ḫubulli *at interest.* 18 [6] 24 [5]

ḫûdu *pleasure.* ḫu-ud 11 [3] 21 [3]

ḫarrânu *business.* 13 [4, 10, 13] 14 [9, 17] 15 [3, 7]

ṭu *shekel.* 11 [5] 13 [1, 7] 14 [4, 6, 7, 10, 14, 15, 16, 17] 18 [1] 19 [1] 20 [1] 22 [1, 5] 24 [4] 25 [1, 3, 10, 13] 26 [1, 7, 8, 9] 27 [6] 28 [1] 30 [1, 9] 31 [4, 5]

ṭâbu *good.* 14 [3, 15]

ki *if.* ki-i 27 [5] *when.* 29 [19]

KI.LU 28 [7]

kalâlu *to be complete.* i-kat-lul 29 [15]

kam Placed after numerals to form ordinals. Very frequent.

kûmu *instead of.* ku-um 11 [4]

ka-pak-i 25 [9]

kasû *cup.* (?) ka-sa-a-ta 14 [11]

kussu *chair.* iṣu kussi 14 [14]

kaspu *silver, money.* Very frequent. kaspi-ia 26 [11] kaspa.a 11 [7] 13 [12] kaspa.a.an 12 [9] 22 [4]

kâru A measure. ka-ru-u 25 [8] ka-ri-śu-nu 25 [9]

karpatu *dish, vessel.* Used as determ. 14 [1]

lâ *not.* 18 [13] 23 [10] 27 [5]

libbu *heart.* lib-bi-śu 11 [3] 21 [3] ina lib-bi *thereupon.* 26 [6]

libittu *brick.* 26 [7]

liḳû *to take.* il-ti-ḳu-u 31 [7]

maḫâru *to receive.* ma-ḫir 28 [6] ma-ḫi-ir 30 [8] maḫ-ḫir 18 [6] ultu ili mi-ḫir-tu *in behalf of.* 18 [4]

mukinnu *witness.* amilu mu-kin-nu 11 [19] 12 [18] 13 [18] 14 [20] 15 [10] 16 [11] 17 [9] 21 [11] 22 [11] 23 [8] 24 [9] (?) 25 [14] 26 [15] 28 [10] 29 [23] 30 [10] 31 [8] amilu mu-kin 27 [5]

mala See the following.

mimma *whatever.* 13 [11] mimma ma-la *as much as.* 13 [4] 15 [3]

mana A piece of money. ma-na 11 [7] 12 [3, 9] 14 [17] 15 [1] 16 [1] 19 [1] 22 [1, 5] 23 [1, 15] 24 [1] 26 [1, 7] 27 [1] ma-ni-i 24 [4] 26 [9] 27 [6]

manû *to count.* ma-nu-u 14 [4, 6]

mandâtu *hire, wages.* man-da-at-tum 16 [6]

manzazu *presence, witness.* 17 [7] 18 [7] 19 [5]

mâru *son.* mâr Frequent. mâr-śu Frequent. amilu mâr śipri *messenger.* 16 [13]

mâru-u-tu *adoption.* 21 [6]

mar.banûtu An official. 11 [10]

marru *hatchet.* mar-ri 14 [12]

martu *daughter*. **marat-su** 16 [3] 22 [9] 26 [?] 28 [3] 29 [6 10]

mu-šaḫ-ḫi-nu A bronze utensil. 14 [10]

maškânu *security, pledge*. **maš-ka-nu** 11 [5] 16 [10] 22 [6] 26 [11 13]

mašâru *to leave behind*. **u-maš-ši-ru** 29 [12]

matu *land*. **mat** Determ. Frequent.

nadânu *to give*. **id-din** 11 [9] 29 [11] **id-di-in** 21 [8] **id-di-nu** 20 [8] 29 [9] **iddin-nu** 17 [8] **id-i-nu** 27 [6] **i-nam-din** 20 [6] 22 [6] 23 [7] 24 [9] **i-nam-di-nu** 16 [7] 29 [18] **na-din** 24 [7] **na-din-na-mu** 12 [11] **li-nad-nu** 21 [9] **na-da-nu** 18 [9] **ina-ad-din** 27 [4] **u-da-nu-tu** 17 [7] **it-ta-din** 29 [20] 31 [7]

namḫaratu A vessel. **nam-ḫa-ra-ta** 14 [2]

namṣâtu A vessel. **nam-ṣa-a-ta** 14 [2]

ni-si-su *bidding*. (?) 29 [16]

naṣâru *to protect*. amilu **ni-ṣur-gi-na** 28 [13 14] (see note.)

našû *to raise*. *To bring*: **na-ši** 11 [11] **na-ša-a-tum** 29 [22] *To take*: **i-na-šu** 15 [7] 16 [8] *To lend*: **na-ša-a-ta** 22 [11]

na-aš-ḫi-ip-ti An iron utensil. 14 [12]

našûttu *command, commission, bidding*. **na-aš-ut-tum** 12 [7] 14 [8] **na-[aš-ut-tu]** 29 [12] **na-aš-ut-ti** 31 [10] 30 [1]

niš-ru 16 [8]

amilu **SA** 13 [4]

sibû An official. 11 [9]

sulûpu *date*. (**ka-lum-ma**) 14 [5]

sipparu *copper*. 14 [10 11] 20 [6]

pânu *face*. *To be received from*: **la-pa-ni** 25 [21] **ina pân** 25 [1 2 5 10 12] *To be at the disposal of*: 14 [19]

paḳirânu An official. 11 [10]

parsillu *iron*. 14 [12 13]

pa-ri-ri-is *female sheep*. (?) 20 [6]

pi-ša-an-na *equal*. 29 [9]

amilu **pa-ši-ki** 15 [12]

pûtu *certificate*. **pu-ut** 11 [9] 24 [9] 29 [21] **pu-u-tu** 15 [6]

ṣabâtu *to take*. **ṣa-bit** 25 [8] **ṣab-ta** 26 [13]

ṣibtu *possession*. **ṣib-tum** 15 [7]

ṣiḫru *small*. **ṣi-ḫi-ri** 21 [4]

ṣiru *plain, field, country*. 25 [10] **ina ali u ṣiri** *in city and country*. 15 [4]

ḳa A measure. 14 [4]

ḳibû *to speak, say*. **iḳ-bi** 11 [8] **iḳ-bu-šu** 21 [8]

amilu **ḳîpu** *guardian, keeper*. 22 [10] 23 [11]

ḳaḳḳadu *head, capital*. 15 [8]

ḳâtû *hand*. **ina ḳâtâ** *from, from the hands of*. 12 [4] 18 [2] 19 [3] 28 [9] 29 [4] 30 [6] **ta-ḳâtâ-miš** See note to 14 [18]

rabû *to become great, increase*. **i-rab-bi** 17 [6] 24 [9] 26 [9] 27 [7] **u-rab-bu-šu** 21 [9]

amilu **rab.ka-a-ri** An official 23 [3] (see note.)

riḫtu *remainder*. **ri-iḫ-tum** 31 [8] **ri-iḫ-ti** 29 [19] **ri-ḫi-it** 23 [16]

riksu *contract*. **ri-ik-su** 12 [13]

riḳu *empty*. **ri-ḳu-tu** 14 [1]

ša *of, which*. Very frequent.

šu 16 [7]

šû *he, it*. **šu-u** 12 [16] 21 [10]

ši.bar *grain*. 25 [20]

šadû *east*. 21 [10]

šidatum *present*. **ši-da-tum** 29 [17]

šaṭâru *to write*. **ša-ṭa-ru** *document*. 31 [7] **ša-ṭa-ra** *in writing*. 29 [13]

šakânu *to place, set*. **šak-na-tum** 11 [5] amilu **šakânu** *governor*. 29 [25]

šikâru *wine*. 14 [3]

šalâmu *to be perfect*. **ša-ta-lam-mu** 14 [10] *to be paid*, hence, *to receive*: **i-šal-li-mu** 22 [8]

šumu *name*. **šu-mu** 15 [7] **šum-šu** 12 [6]

šîmu *price*. 11 [7] 12 [4 10] 28 [4] 29 [8]

šanû *to change*. **ša-a-na-a-na** *neither*. 13 [8] **ši-na** *double*. 18 [3]

šangu *priest*. amilu **šangu** 16 [4 17] 17 [10 12] 18 [9] 24 [12] 25 [13 18] 30 [3 6]

šipru *message*. amilu **mâr šipri** *messenger*. 16 [13]

šarâḳu *to present.* **i-šar-ra-ku** 29 [17]

šarru *king.* 23 [3, 16] **šar** 11 [21] 12 [22] 13 [19] 14 [27] 15 [15] 16 [19] 17 [5, 16] 18 [19] 19 [11] 20 [16] 21 [22] 22 [17] 23 [14] 24 [16] 25 [19] 26 [24] 27 [14] 28 [17] 29 [20] 30 [17] 31 [12]

šattu *year.* 11 [20] 12 [21] 13 [18] 14 [20] 15 [6, 14] 16 [7, 18] 17 [5, 18] 18 [16] 19 [18] 20 [14] 21 [21] 22 [17] 23 [13] 24 [15] 25 [10] 26 [22] 27 [14] 28 [16] 29 [20] 30 [16] 31 [12] **šatta** *every year.* 31 [4] **šanâti** *two years.* 19 [3]

ta Placed after numerals. 14 [3, 11, 14, 15] 19 [3] **ta-ḳâtâ-miš** See note to 14 [16] **ta.a.an** 31 [7]

tibnu *straw.* 14 [13]

ti-lit-tum *amount.* (?) 18 [3]

târu *to turn, return.* **u-tir** 29 [19] **ti-ra** 26 [11] **ti-ra-šu** 26 [12]

NO. 11.

FRONT.

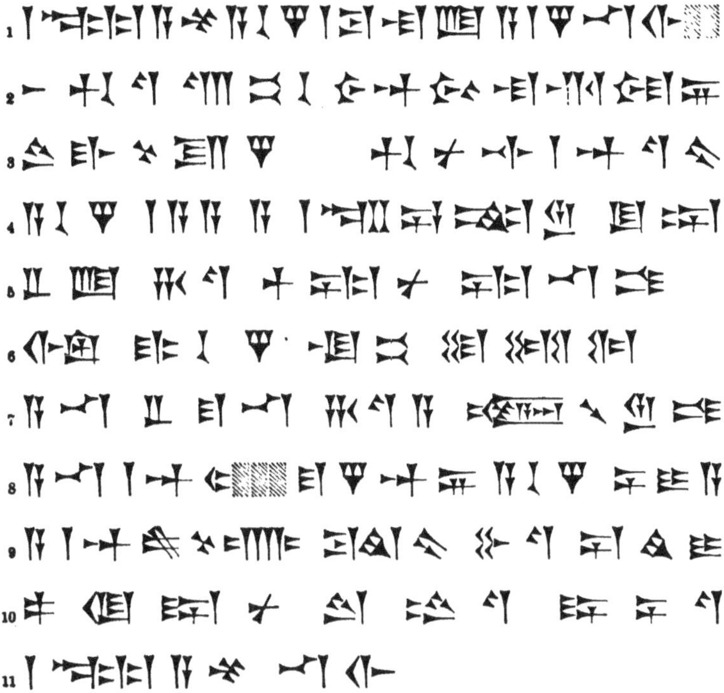

BACK.

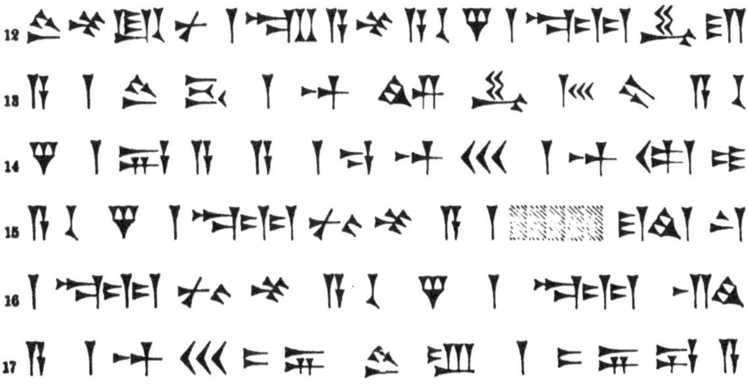

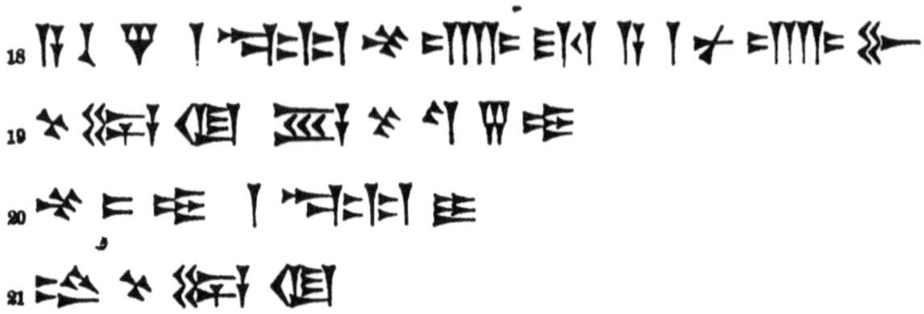

Tablet of a light brown color, 1⅝ x 2¼ inches. There are numerous breaks upon it, and many of the signs of the first five lines of the reverse are filled with a hard flinty substance, rendering the decipherment difficult. The four edges are not written upon.

Transliteration.	*Translation.*
1 Nabû-apal-iddin apal-šu ša Ba-la-ṭu apal Ša-na-ši-......	1 Nabûapaliddin, the son of Balatu, the son of Shanashe......
2 ina ḫu-ud lib-bi-šu Gu-la-ri-nin-ni	2 in the pleasure of his heart, Gularininni
3 amilu gal-lat-su ša Ḫu-nu-ti-tiš-Šamaš-balaṭu	3 his slave, — whom Hunutitishshamashbalatu,
4 apal-šu ša Ai apal Bil-i-ṭi-ru ku-um	4 the son of Ai, the son of Beletèru, instead of
5 1/3 ṭu kaspi maš-ka-nu šak-na-tum	5 one third shekel of money as security had set, —
6 u mar-šu ša aḳ-bi tu-li-di	6 and her child, whom he said she will give birth to,
7 a-na 1/3 ma-na kaspa.a šim gam-ru-tum	7 for one third mana of money, the full price,
8 a-na [Marduk]-iḳi-ša-an-ni apal-šu ša Bani-i-a	8 to Mardukikishânni, the son of Bania,
9 apal Îllatu-u iddin pu-ut si-ḫi-i	9 the son of Ellatû, gave. The certificate of the sihi,
10 pa-ḳi-ra-nu arad-šarrû-tu mar-banû-tu	10 the pakiranu, the arad-sharrûtu (and) the mar-banûtu officials,
11 Nabû-apal-iddin na-ši.	11 Nabûapaliddin will bring.
12 amilu mu-kin-nu Bil-apal-iddin apal-šu ša Nabû-aḫi-irba	12 Witnesses: Belapaliddin, the son of Nabûahirba,
13 apal Ḳur(?)-ban Rammânu-aḫi-uballiṭ apal-šu	13 the son of Kurban; Rammânuahîuballit, the son
14 ša Dan-a apal Nûr-Sin Nirgal-na'id	14 of Dana, the son of Nûrsin; Nergalna'id,
15 apal-šu ša Nabû-zir-iddin apal ...-it-ḳa	15 the son of Nabûziriddin, the son of ... .itka;
16 Nabû-zir-iddin apal-šu ša Nabû-	16 Nabûziriddin, the son of Nabûmusallim,

musallim	
17 **apal Sin-tab-ni** amilu **dupsar Tab-ni-i-a**	17 the son of Sintabni. Scribe: Tabnêa,
18 **apal-šu ša Nabû-mu-u-da apal Nu-u-pu**	18 the son of Nabûmûda, the son of Nûpu.
19 **Babilu araḫ Adaru ûmu 5 kam**	19 Babylon, in the month Adar, on the 5 th day,
20 **šattu 2 kam Nabû-na'id**	20 in the 2 nd year of Nabûna'id,
21 **šar 'Babili**	21 King of Babylon.

NOTES.

2. **ina ḫu-ud lib-bi-šu.** A legal phrase. See Peiser's explanation in Z. A. III, 70. — 3. The space in the line indicates an erasure on the tablet by the scribe. He probably, by mistake, also erased the perpendicular wedge that usually introduces a person's name. — 5. **šak-na-tum.** This form occurs also Strass. Nabn. 253, 10. — 6. A very condensed expression. It is peculiar to find the form **aḳ-bi** used here instead of **iḳ-bi.** We would expect the third person; the sense evidently requires it: I have therefore translated it thus. The same form occurs in Strass. Nabn. 1113, 18 and 720, 10. I would class it as one of those mistakes so common in colloquial language. Or else, it might be taken as an instance where the dictator of the tablet has fallen out of his role, and has used the first instead of the third person. — 8. Undoubtedly M a r d u k, as the first signs show. Before the name **Bani-i-ia,** the determinative for person is again omitted. — 10. **pa-ḳi-ra-nu** is also used to denote the plaintiff, or the one that objects to the business transaction. But here it refers to an official. I would take **arad-šarrûtu** and **mar-banûtu** as officials in charge of the slave trade. Oppert, however, strenuously objects to this rendering (Z. A. III, 178). — 12. The sign **kin,** as will be seen, is written in a great variety of ways. I have endeavored in the texts to give them as near the actual writing as my type permits. — 13. The sign for **ḳur** is strange; the horizontal wedge ought to have been omitted. Perhaps it is a mistake on the part of the scribe. **Ḳurban** means "gift" and may well be compared with the Hebrew קָרְבָּן Neh. x:35; xiii:31. Compare also קָרְבָּן Lev. vii:38, the Arabic قُرْبَان "sacrifice, offering", and the Greek κορβᾶν Mark vii:11. — 20. Therefore the tablet is dated in the year 553 B. C.

Hunutitishshamashbalatu owed Nabuapaliddin ⅓ shekel of money. He evidently could not pay. So he gave his slave Gularininni, who was pregnant, to the latter as security. Now Nabuapaliddin had no use for the slave, or he saw that he could make a good bargain. Therefore, becoming tired of waiting, he resolves to sell the slave and her unborn child. He sells at an immense profit, — (or he is required to return the difference in the two amounts to the owner of the slave). The certificate of the officials, mentioned in lines 9 and 10, was obtained in order that there might be no dispute about the ownership of the slaves.

NO. 12.

FRONT.

BACK.

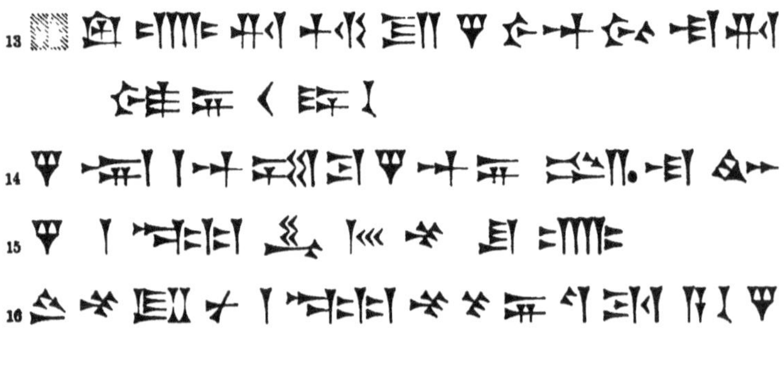

This beautiful tablet is of a dark yellow color, with large spots of brick red upon it. Size 1 5/8 x 2 1/4 inches. The writing on it is very clear, though some of the signs, especially in the first, second, and tenth lines, are run very closely together. The upper edge and the edges of the two sides are not written upon. The corners are slightly damaged, yet the signs can be clearly distinguished.

Transliteration.	*Translation.*
1 **Gu-la-ri-nin-ni u mar-šu**	1 Gularininni and her son,
2 **ša Marduk-iḳi-ša-an-ni apal-šu ša Ba-ni-ia**	2 whom Mardukikishânni, the son of Bania,
3 **apal ......-uṣur-bilu-u a-na 2/3 ma-na kaspi**	3 the son of ..... usurbelû, for two thirds mana of money,
4 **a-na šim gam-ru-tu ina ḳâtâ Nabû-apal-iddin**	4 at the full price, from the hands of Nabûapaliddin,
5 **apal-šu ša Îṭir-ša-na-nim i-pu-šu**	5 the son of Etêrshananim, received;
6 **u u.an.tim a-na šum-šu i-'-i-li**	6 and a receipt in his name he set up,
7 **ina na-aš-ut-tum ša Nabû-aḫi-iddin**	7 at the bidding of Nabûahiddin,
8 **apal-šu ša Šu-la-a apal Î-gi-bi**	8 the son of Shulâ, the son of Egibi.
9 **kaspa.a.an 2/3 ma-na ... ša Nabû-aḫi-iddin**	9 In money two thirds mana . . . , which Nabûahiddin
10 **a-na šim Gu-la-ri-nin-ni u mar-šu**	10 for the price of Gularininni and her son
11 **a-na Nabû-apal-iddin na-din-na-mu**	11 unto Nabûapaliddin gave.
12 **u.an.tim gab-ri u.an.tim**	12 The duplicate receipt, the .... receipt
13 **... -lu-u ri-ik-su ša Gu-la-ri-nin-ni u mar-šu**	13 (and) the contract tablet about Gularininni and her son,
14 **ša dupsar Marduk-iḳi-ša-an-ni il-la-'**	14 which the scribe (for) Mardukikishânni had set up,
15 **ša Nabû-aḫi-iddin šu-u**	15 the possession of Nabûahiddin it is.
16 **amilu mu-kin-nu Nabû-mu-ši-ni-ud-da apal-šu ša**	16 Witnesses: Nabûmusheniudda, the son of

17 Bil-śu-nu apal Bil-pat-ta-nu	17 Belshunu, the son of Belpattanu;
18 Ki-di-nu apal-śu śa Marduk-iṭi-ir	18 Kidinu, the son of Marduketêr,
19 apal Rammân-u-mi-i u amilu dupsar Bil-kaṣir apal-śu	19 the son of Rammânumê; and the scribe Belkasir, the son
20 śa Bil-ri-man-ni apal Ba-bu-tu	20 of Belrimanni, the son of Babutu.
21 Babilu araḫ Adaru ûmu 22 kam śattu 2 kam	21 Babylon, in the month Adar, on the 22nd day, in the 2nd year of
22 Nabû-na'id śar Babili.	22 Nabûna'id, King of Babylon.

NOTES.

3. In the break here the last sign would indicate that either N e r g a l or M a r d u k has been broken off. — 5. Literally, "he made", then, "he received". — 6. As it was no concern of Mardukikishanni who would ultimately possess his slaves, the receipt was naturally made out in the name of the present purchaser, Nabûapaliddin. — 7. na-aś-ut-tum, as Tallqvist reads the word, taking it from the root naśû. Peiser, on the other hand, reads na-aś-pir-tum, taking it from the root śapâru, "to send". Either is admissible. The former reading is chosen here because, to my judgment, it is the better. — 8. If the break contains ina ili, the following śa must be read ḫi (the appearance of the sign on the tablet would admit either) and the whole would be ina muḫḫi. This would not materially alter the sense, we would only have to supply "it" at the end of line 11. The passage would then read: "Two thirds of a mana to be received from N. for the price of G. and her son: to N. he gave it." Notice the form na-din-na-mu from nadânu. — 12. The first u.an.tim and gabri must be read together, and the second u.an. tim. with the illegible adjective in line 13. — 13. 14. This contract evidently gave age, parentage and history of the slaves, together with the certificate of the officials appointed by the government to take charge of the slave tradè. This naturally went to the purchaser, so that he could have, so to speak, a legal document showing his right to the slaves. — 14. A very unusual form for Marduk, the usual form is given in lines 2 and 18. — 15. śu-u refers to the contract tablet described in 13. 14. — 21. Hence in the year 553 B. C.

This tablet treats of a sale through commission. Nabuahidin, one of the Egibi family, has instructed Mardukikishani, his agent probably, to purchase for him the slave Gularininni and her boy from Nabuapaliddin. The last named receives the full price from Mardukikishani, who in turn receives the purchase money from the original purchaser. We therefore appropriately find in line 12 mention made of a duplicate receipt, as each of the purchasers wished to be safe from all insinuations that the money had not been properly paid. Finally, Nabuahiddin, into whose possession the two slaves had now passed, becomes the possessor also of all the tablets bearing upon the sale.

NO. 13.

FRONT.

BACK.

Small tablet of a brown color, 1¼ x 2 inches. The signs are very plain with two exceptions, one in the 5th and the other in the 17th line. It is but slightly damaged at the two lower corners of the obverse.

Transliteration.	*Translation.*
1 1/3 ṭu kaspi ša Rimut apal-šu ša	1 ⅓ shekel of money which Rimut, the son of
2 Ḳur-ban-ni-Marduk apal Îpi-iš-ilu	2 Kurbanimarduk, the son of Epêshilu,
3 ina ili Bil-iddin apal-šu ša Nirgal-uballi-iṭ	3 is to receive from Beliddin, the son of Nergaluballit,
4 apal amilu sa a-na ḫarrâni mimma ma-la	4 the son of the ... In regard to business, as much as he
5 ina alû Kas-sur(?) ip-pu-uš-šu a-ḫi	5 in the city Kassur gains, a share
6 ina u-tur Bil-iddin it-ti Ri-mut	6 in the profit Beliddin with Rimut
7 ik-kal ul-tu ili 1 ṭu kaspi	7 will consume. Below 1 shekel of money
8 ša-a-na-a-na ul i-ti-iḳ	8 neither shall take away.
9 ša i-ti-iḳ a-na ili il-li	9 Who does take (anything) away, against (him) there is a debt.
10 Bil-iddin na-aš-ut-ti ša ḫarrâni	10 Beliddin the command of the business
11 il-lak mimma i-lat ša Bil-iddin	11 possesses. Whatever is additional, belonging to Beliddin
12 ia-a-nu kaspu ša ḫarrâni ša Nabû-aḫi-iddin	12 it is not. The capital of the business belongs to Nabûahiddin.
13 amilu mu-kin-nu Ri-mut apal-šu ša Ni-mi-ḳu	13 Witnesses: Rimut, the son of Nimeku,
14 apal Man-di-di Arad-Bil apal-šu ša	14 the son of Mandidi; Aradbel, the son of
15 Du-um-muḳ apal Arad-Bil	15 Dûmmuk, the son of Aradbel.
16 amilu dupsar Nabû-apal-iddin apal-šu ša Da-bi-ia	16 Scribe: Nabûapaliddin, the son of Dabia,
17 apal Šu-ḫa-ai Babilu araḫ Tašritu	17 the son of Subâ. Babylon, in the month Tashrit,
18 ûmu 22 kam šattu 4 kam Nabû-na'id	18 on the 22nd day, in the 4th year of Nabûna'id,
19 šar Babili	19 King of Babylon.

NOTES.

2. **Ḳur-ban-ni-Marduk** occurs also in the next tablet (14, 19), but the syllable **ni** is omitted. Undoubtedly the same man is mentioned in both cases. For **Ḳur-ban** see 11, 13. **Išišilu** Cf. the Hebrew עשהאל. — 5. Beginning of line 5 is blurred; therefore the reading of the name **alû Kassur** can be but tentative. — 6. **u-tur** I would connect with **atru** "more, exceeding"; and **atâru** "to be above". Compare also the Hebrew יותר "that which remains over", then, "profit". The word occurs also in 15, 5. — 7. Literally "will eat", the meaning is "will share". **ultu ili**, a phrase not common in the contract tablets. Cf. **ištu ili** Del. Gram. § 81*b*. It has the sense here, undoubtedly, of "from, below". — 8. **ša-a-na-a-na** "the other", then in a wider sense, "either". **i-ti-iḳ**, from **itiḳu** "to remove", but here spelled with the *i* and not the *e* vowel. — 9. **il-li** "to be as a burden or debt", from **ilû** "to go up". The word occurs in this form in Strass. Nbk. 300, 10. After **ili** we must supply **šu**, which is often omitted. — 10. **na-aš-ut-ti**: see note to 12, 7. — 11. **il-lak** from **alâku**. The phrase **našû'a alâku** (Tallq. p. 108) means "to go at the bidding of, to perform a business transaction for"; here, I take it, the sense requires another translation. **i-lat** (Phœnecian עלת Schröder, Phœn. Gram. § 120) is an adverbial form from עלה. See Z. A. III, 71. 175; Tallq. p. 40. **ia-a-nu**, compare the Hebrew אין. — 15. The large space in the middle of the line indicates an erasure by the scribe on the tablet. The traces of the word he had written would give us for the first sign **amilu**, as in line 16. The scribe forgot, at first, to record the last witnesses family name in his anxiety to have enough room for his own name. — 17. The sign for **ḫa** is doubtful. — 18. Dated in the year 551 B. C.

Beliddin and Rimut have gone into partnership with a certain sum of money advanced by Nabuahiddin. Beliddin is to manage the business, while Rimut is to do the work in a certain city. Beforehand Beliddin is to pay ½ shekel to Rimut, perhaps in order to induce him to enter the partnership, or to pay off a debt. Both are to share in the profit *equally*, otherwise there would be a statement to the contrary. This division is to take place only when the profit amounts to more than one shekel. If either anticipates and takes his share beforehand, he is in debt by this amount to his partner. On account of the smallness of the amounts involved, it may be supposed that the contract is one between two humble mechanics, perhaps weavers or gardeners.

NO. 14.

FRONT.

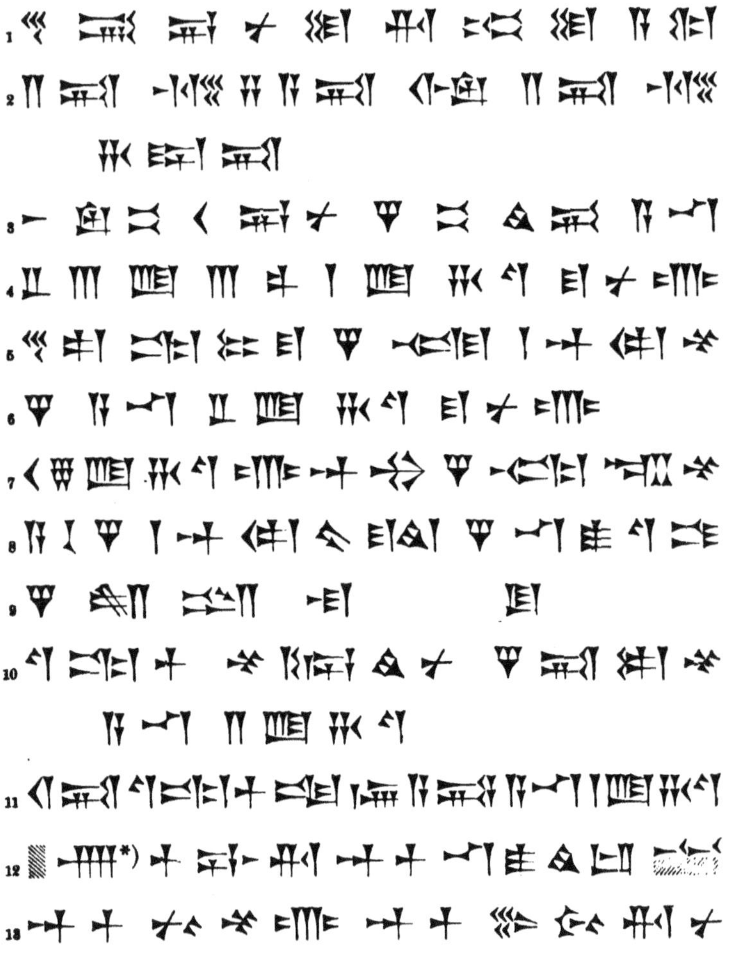

BACK.

*) This sign I would rather read *u* instead of *nun* or *sil*. The horizontal wedge is made so deep that it may accidentally have covered the second horizontal wedge of the sign *u*.

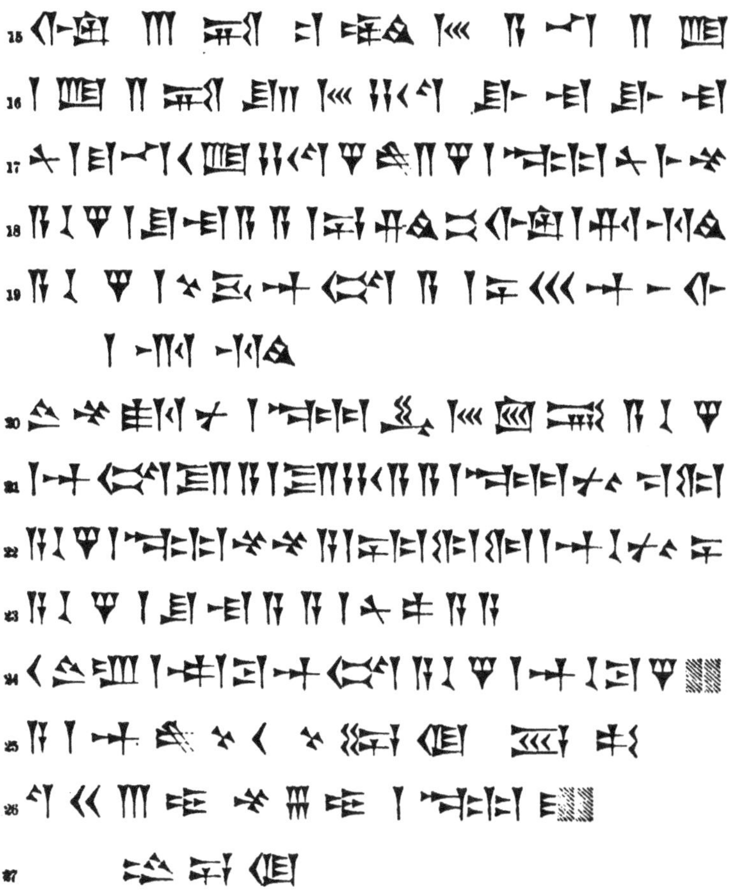

Tablet of a light brown color, 2 x 2⅓ inches. The upper and lower sides are well-curved, while the right and the left sides are perfectly flat. The signs are very plain and clearly made. There is a small space after line 27 dividing the writing, otherwise the latter goes around the tablet continuously. The sides contain no writing.

Transliteration.	*Translation.*
1 40 karpatu dan-nu-tu ri-ḳu-tu a-di	1 40 empty vessels together with
2 2 ta nam-ṣa-a-ta u 2 ta nam-ḫa-ra-ta	2 2 . . . . . . vessels; 2 sacrificial vessels
3 ina dib-bi 10 dan-nu ša šikâri ṭâbi a-na	3 (pending) in suit; 10 vessels of good wine to the value of
4 1/3 [ḳa] 3 ṭu 3 ḳa 1 ṭu kaspi ma-nu-u	4 ⅓ ka for 3 shekels, — 3 ka (equivalent to) 1 shekel to be counted; —

5 40 mašiḫu(?) sulûpi ša ina ili Nirgal-iddin	5 40 measures of dates, which are to be received from Nergaliddin,
6 ša a-na 1/3 ṭu kaspi ma-nu-u	6 which to the value of 1/3 shekel of money are to be counted;
7 18 ṭu kaspi u.an.tim ša ina ili Bil-iddin	7 18 shekels of money, a receipt for which is to be received from Beliddin,
8 apal-šu ša Nirgal-uballi-iṭ ša na-aš-ut-tum	8 the son of Nergaluballit, who the command
9 ša ḫarrâni il-la-ku	9 of the business possesses.
10 sipparu mu-šaḫ-ḫi-nu ša-ta-lam-mu a-na 2 ṭu kaspi	10 A perfect copper ...... to the value of 2 shekels of money;
11 11 ta sipparu ka-sa-a-ta a-na 1 ṭu kaspi	11 11 copper cups(?) to the value of 1 shekel of money;
12 ......-u-bar mar-ri parzili na-aš-ḫi-ip-ti	12 ...... an iron hatchet; an iron ......;
13 parzili zir-mu-u parzili tibnu gu-ri-nu	13 an iron ......; threshed(?) straw
14 a-na 2 ṭu 4 ta iṣu kussi	14 to the value of 2 shekels; 4 chairs;
15 u 3 ta iṣu iṣu ṭâbu(?) a-na 2 ṭu	15 and 3 good logs of wood(?) to the value of 2 shekels;
16 1 ṭu 2 ta ḳâtâ-miš kaspi gal-la gal-la	16 1 and ⅔ shekels of money; slaves;
17 1/2 1 ma-na 10 ṭu kaspi ša ḫarrâni ša Nabû-aḫi-iddin	17 1½ mana, 10 shekels of money in the business of Nabûahiddin,
18 apal-šu ša Šu-la-a apal Î-gi-bi u Ri-mut	18 the son of Shulâ, the son of Egibi, and of Rimut,
19 apal-šu ša Ḳur-ban-Marduk apal Îpi-iš-ilu ina pâni Ri-mut	19 the son of Kurbanmarduk, the son of Epêshilu, are at the disposal of Rimut.
20 amilu mu-kin-nu Nabû-aḫi-bul-luṭ apal-šu ša	20 Witnesses: Nabûahibullut, the son of
21 Marduk-irba apal Šu-ḫa-ai Nabû-zir-šutišur	21 Mardukirba, the son of Suhâ; Nabûzirshuteshur,
22 apal-šu ša Nabû-šum-iddin apal Ka-di-di Marduk-zir-ibni	22 the son of Nabûshumiddin, the son of Kadidi; Mardukziribni,
23 apal-šu ša Šu-la-a apal Naṣir-ḫat-ai	23 the son of Shulâ, the son of Nasirhatâ;
24 u amilu dupsar Irba-Marduk apal-šu ša Marduk-iḳi-ša-[an-ni]	24 and the scribe Irbamarduk, the son of Mardukikishanni,
25 apal Îllatu-u Babilu araḫ Airu	25 the son of Ellatu. Babylon, in the month Airu,
26 ûmu 23 kam šattu 6 kam Nabû-na'id	26 on the 23rd day, in the 6th year of Nabûna'id,
27 šar Babili	27 King of Babylon.

NOTES.

1. **riḳutu** must be connected with רִיק "empty." — 2. **namṣata** is mentioned also (**nam-ṣa-tum**) in Strass., Nabn. 258, 12; Peiser, Bab. Ver. CXLIII, 11; Haupt, B. A. I, 176. **namḫarata**. Cf. Lotze, TP 1:5. This word occurs again in Strass., Nabn. 258, 13; 767, 13; Cyr. 183, 18; also in Peiser, Bab. Ver. CXLVIII, 14. — 3. **dib-bi** means "suit, complaint before a court." For other instances see Tallq. p. 63. **šikari ṭâbi**. Consult Peiser, Bab. Ver. p. 249. For the different varieties of wine see Zehnpfund's excellent notes in B. A. I, p. 524, note ***, and his addition to this note on pp. 634, 635. — 4. This line seems to say that the wine shall be rated at a reduced price. — 5. The sign for **mašiḫu** is uncertain. Cf. Peiser, K. A. p. 101; Bab. Ver. p. 243. — 9. It seems as if the sign for **ṭu** had been written on the tablet instead of **ḫarrânu** at first. — 10. **mu-šaḫ-ḫi-nu**. Tallqvist on page 132 suggests "a utensil of bronze." **ša-ta-lam-mu** must be taken from the root **šalâmu** "to be perfect." — 11. **kasâta** may be the Hebrew כּוֹס — 12. **marri** "hatchet." Tallqvist on page 97 fully explains the derivation and meaning of the word. Zehnpfund, however, in B. A. I, p. 535 and 636 objects to this translation. He treats **marru** as a synonym of **ungu** "ring." **našḫipti** is some utensil made of iron. The word occurs also in Strass., Nabn. 571, 15; 784, 2; 926, 4; Peiser, Bab. Ver., p. 305. — 13. **si:-mu-u** also in Strass., Nabn. 258, 36. **tibnu** occurs also, but spelled out, in Strass., Nabn. 231, 3. **gu-ri-nu** may be connected with the Hebrew גֹּרֶן "threshing floor." Hence **tibnu gurinu** may mean "threshed straw." — 16. That **ḳâtâ-miš** is added to numerals in order to denote fractions, the denominator of which is one number higher than the given number, and that the latter forms the numerator, is conclusively shown in the "Sitzungsbericht d. Kgl. Ak. d. Wissensch. zu Berlin," 1889, p. 828, Anm. 1. — 17. **galla galla** is the old way of writing the plural. — 19. **Ḳu:-ban-Marduk** is the same person that is mentioned in 13, 2, which see. **ina pân** is an idiomatic expression, meaning "to be received from," (cf. 25, 1. 2. 5. 10. 12.); but **ina pâni**, here, means "to be at the disposal of, to be the property of." — 20. **bul-luṭ**. The usual form is **bul-liṭ**; the **u** of **bul** has evidently attracted the vowel in **luṭ**. — 25. **Îllatu-u** (also 11, 9) is also given in Strass., "Wörterver. z. d. Inschrift. z. Liverpool." p. 20. — 26. Undoubtedly **na'id**, as the first three wedges show. Tablet dated in the year 549 B. C.

Nabuahiddin, and Rimut had formed a partnership. They determined to give up their joint business. Nabuahiddin, therefore, makes out a list of the articles and the money that are to fall to the share of Rimut. There we find copper, iron, and wooden utensils mentioned, and their respective values given; spices, wine, and money added, and all handed over to Rimut. Even Beliddin, their business manager, is compelled to pay back to Rimut the money he loaned from the latter.

It is to be regretted that we know so little about the various vessels and implements mentioned here. The value attached to each, however, shows them to be small and common objects.

NO. 15.

FRONT.

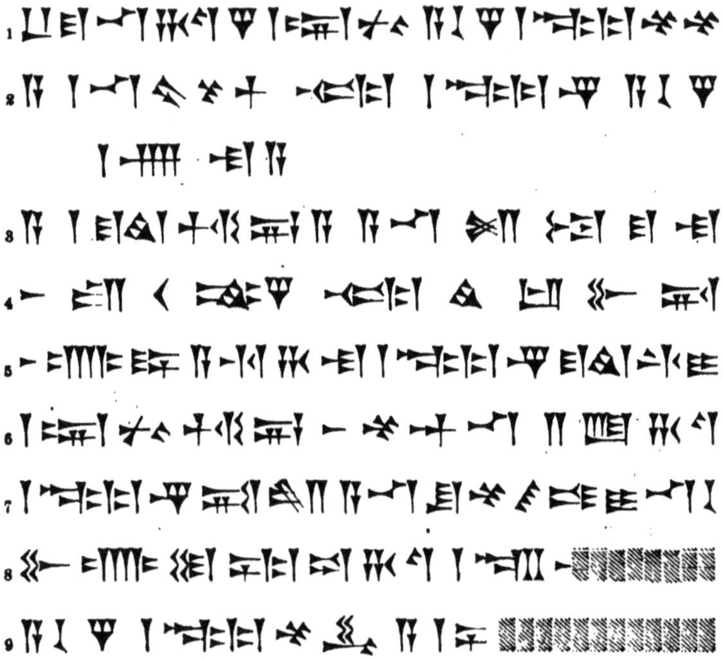

BACK.

Tablet of a light brown color. 1⅝ x 2⅛ inches. The tablet is gradually crumbling off, and it is fortunate that this copy could be made before the signs have been effaced. The right hand lower corner of the obverse is broken off, and thus the last signs of lines 8, 9, 10, and 11 are destroyed. The writing is plain and well defined. The left side is without inscription. There is also a large space between lines 12 and 13.

Transliteration.	*Translation.*
1 1/3 ma-na kaspi ša Šapik-zir apal-šu ša Nabû-šum-iddin	1 ⅓ mana of money, which Shapikzir, the son of Nabûshumiddin,
2 apal Na-din-ši-bar ina ili Nabû-iṭir apal-šu ša Ṣil-la-a	2 the son of Nadinshebar, is to receive from Nabûetêr, the son of Sillâ,
3 apal It-ik-kal-la a-na ḫarrâni mimma ma-la	3 the son of Itikkala, for the business, so much
4 ina ali u ṣi-ri ina ili ip-pu-uš	4 in city and country from (him) he will acquire.
5 ina u-tur a-ḫu sittu Nabû-iṭir it-ti-i	5 In the profit a part — the joint possession — Nabûetêr with
6 Šapik-zir ik-kal ina šatti 2 ṭu kaspi	6 Shapikzir will consume; during the year 2 shekels of money
7 Nabû-iṭir ultu ḫarrâni a-na šu-mu ṣib-tum i-na-šu	7 Nabûetêr from the business upon (his) name, as possession, will take.
8 pu-u-tu ḳaḳḳadi kaspi Bîl-......	8 The receipt for the principal of money Bel......
9 apal-šu ša Nabû-šum-uṣur apal Bani-[ia]	9 the son of Nabûshumusur, the son of Bania, (has received).
10 amilu mu-kin-nu Nabû-balaṭ-su-[iḳ-bi apal-šu ša]	10 Witnesses: Nabûbalatsuikbi, the son of
11 Zir-ia apal amilu bânû Nabû-ukin-[zir]	11 Ziria, the son of the carpenter; Nabûkinzir,
12 apal-šu ša Bîl-uballi-iṭ apal amilu pa-ši-ki	12 the son of Beluballit, the son of the ... man;
13 amilu ṭupšar Bîl-uballi-iṭ apal-šu ša Na-di-nu	13 the scribe Beluballit, the son of Nadin.
14 Babilu araḫ Samna ûmu 11 kam šattu 6 kam	14 Babylon, in the month Marcheshwan, on the 11 th day, in the 6 th year of
15 Nabû-na'id šar Babili	15 Nabûna'id, King of Babylon.

NOTES.

3. The vertical wedge at the beginning of the sign **mimma** is left out. — 4. **ip-pu-uš**, "has acquired." **ipišu** has this meaning also in Deluge Tablets, l. 277. **ina ali u ṣiri**. This phrase occurs also in Peiser, Bab. Ver. XXXVIII, 8. See also Tallqvist, p. 120. — 5. **u-tur**, see note to 9, 6. Also Strass., Cyr. 148, 7; Nbk. 51, 4. — 7. **i-na-šu**. Similar forms occur in Strass., Nabn. 63, 12; 746, 14; Nbk. 235, 9. **ṣibtum** from

ṣabâtu "to take." "The term is generally used to denote possessions of clothing and other articles, but here also of money. See Tallqvist, p. 120 and 121. — 8. pu-u-tu. This adds another form to Peiser's much discussed puṭ and Tallqvist's bud. Abel and Winckler, on p. 81*b* of their Keilschrifttexte, give a word pûtu "Zugang", which may be connected with the above. — 9. Nabû-šum-uṣur. Another sign had previously been written for uṣur, but was changed to its present form. — 11. amîlu bânû (GIM). See Tallqvist, p. 57 and 61. — 12. amîlu pa-ši-ki. For other passages see Tallqvist, p. 118; also his note. — 14. Dated in the year 540 B. C., as the preceding tablet.

Shapikzir and Nabueter have made a business venture together. Besides the little money they invested, they borrowed as capital to work with a certain amount of money from Bel......, the son of Nabushum-usur. Now, there had been some disagreement, and the partners sought to frame this document, as an agreement explaining their relations toward one another. Nabueter is thus shown to be ⅓ of a mana in debt to Nabushumiddin, which sum he covers by real estate in the city and in the country. In the profit derived from their business, both are to have an equal share, excepting that Nabueter is to have an additional amount of two shekels, by virtue of some service (not explained in this tablet) rendered. This sum is to be paid upon his name; that is, he is to give a receipt for this money independent of the firm-name, he alone receiving the money.

NO. 16.

FRONT.

BACK.

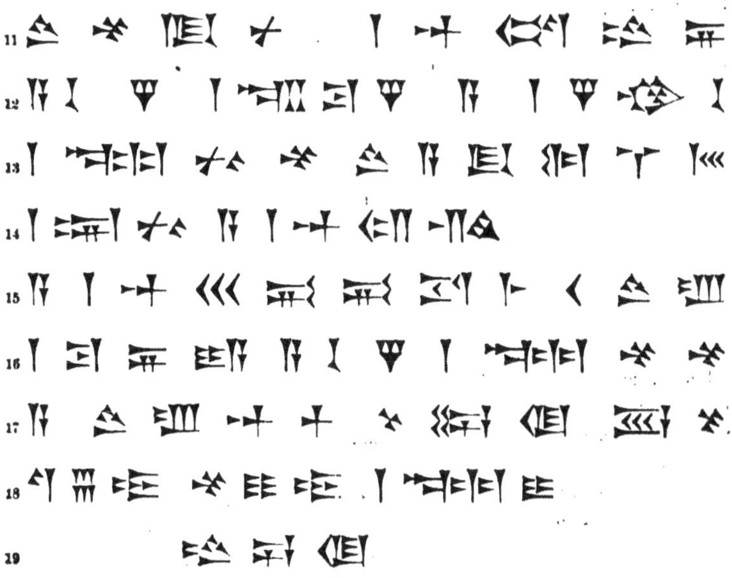

Tablet is of a dark brown color. the reverse is almost black; 1⅜ x 1⅞ inches, and rectangular. The signs are not very distinct. The left and right sides are not written upon.

Transliteration.	*Translation.*
1 1/3 ma-na kaspi ša Bani-a-tu-Î-sag-ila	1 ⅓ mana of money which Baniatuesagila,
2 marat-su ša Nabû-šum-iddin	2 daughter of Nabûshumiddin,
3 ina ili Ba-ni-ia apal-šu ša Nabû-šum-iddin	3 is to receive from Bania, the son of Nabûshumiddin,
4 apal amilu šangu Ninip u Ra-mu-u-a	4 the son of the priest of Ninip, and of Ramûa,
5 aššati-šu kaspu man-da-at-tum	5 his wife. The money is the wages

6 ša Si-nu-nu aš-šat-ti 10 ṭu kaspi	6 of Sinunu the servant. 10 shekels of money
7 i-nam-di-nu a-di 3 šu šatta	7 they will give, together with 3 shu a year,
8 u niš-ru gab-bu-tu 2 i-na-šu	8 and the entire sum (?) the two will bring.
9 Ḫa-an-na-'-šu aš-šat-su-nu	9 Hâna'shu their maid-servant
10 maš-ka-nu ša Bani-a-tu-Î-sag-ila	10 is the security of Baniatuesagila.
11 amilu mu-kin-nu Ma-duk-šarrâ-ni	11 Witness: Mardukshatrâni,
12 apal-šu ša Bil-iḳi-ša apal Ša-tâb i-šu	12 the son of Belikisha, the son of Shatâbtishu;
13 Nabû-zir-iddin amilu mâr šipri daini	13 Nabûziriddin, the messenger of the judges;
14 Šapik-zir apal Nirgal-musallim	14 Shapikzir, the son of Nergalmusallim,
15 apal Sin-ga-ga-nim-mi u amilu dupsar	15 the son of Singaganimme; and the scribe
16 Ba-ni-ia apal-šu ša Nabû-šum-iddin	16 Bania, the son of Nabûshumiddin,
17 apal amilu šangu Ninip Babilu araḫ Adaru	17 the son of the priest of Ninip. Babylon, in the month Adar,
18 ûmu 6 kam šattu 6 kam Nabû-na'id	18 on the 6th day of the 6th year of Nabûna'id,
19 šar Babili	19 King of Babylon.

NOTES.

1. **Baniatu.** A form from the root **banû** "to build." Hence, probably, "daughter." Compare the Hebrew בנה "to beget," Gen. xxx: 3. **Isagila** was the name of the temple of Marduk at Babylon (Z. A. II, p. 179; Tiele, Babylonisch-Assyrische Geschichte, p. 541; Jensen, Cosmologie p. 492; Hommel, Babylonisch-Assyrische Geschichte p. 230; Sayce, Babylonian Religion, p. 64). Hence the name implies that she was born or lived in its neighborhood. — 6. **aššattu** here has the meaning of "servant, slave." It generally means "wife." — 7. The sign **šu** is often taken to be **šanitu** "time." Jensen (Cosmologie p. 4?7), however, doubts it; also Winckler in A. & W. Keilschrifttexte, Schrifttafel No. 347. Here it is some article. If **šu** is to be read **šanitu**, Bania and his wife seem to agree to pay the remaining 10 shekels (1 mana = 60 shekels, ⅓ mana = 20 shekels; 10 they pay immediately, leaving 10 to be paid) in three installments during the year. For the word **šattu** see Pognon, L'inscription de Bavian, p. 168. — 8. **niš-ru** must have the meaning of "sum" or "debt" in this passage; cf. Taliq. p. 108. It is curious that the simple numeral, two vertical wedges, suffices to denote the "two" persons. — 14. The scribe wrote **apal** instead of **apal-šu ša**; the latter usually precedes the father's name, while the former precedes the family name. Some other reason, however, may have prompted this omission. — 18. Dated in the year 549 B. C., as the two preceding tablets.

Baniatuesagila had loaned her brother, the priest of Ninip, and his wife her slave Sinunu for 20 shekels wages. Bania was not rich enough to pay the amount immediately, so he paid 10 shekels at once and promised to pay the remainder during the year. Until this agreement had been complied with, the slave of Bania and his wife was to remain as security with his sister. Even among so closely related members of a family legal forms had to be complied with!

NO. 17.

FRONT.

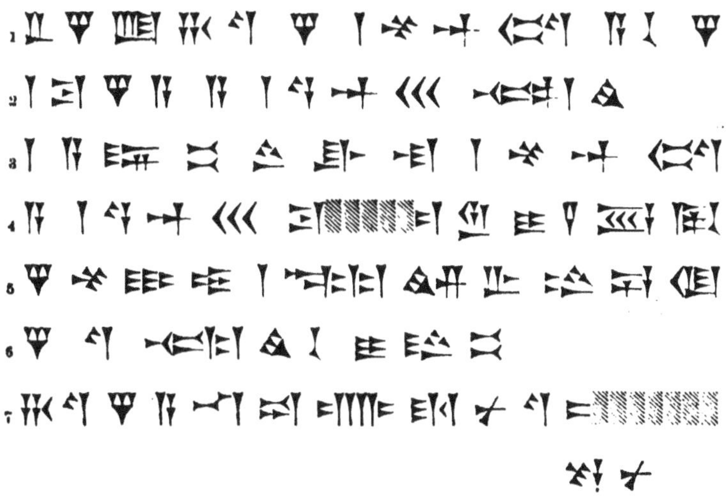

BACK.

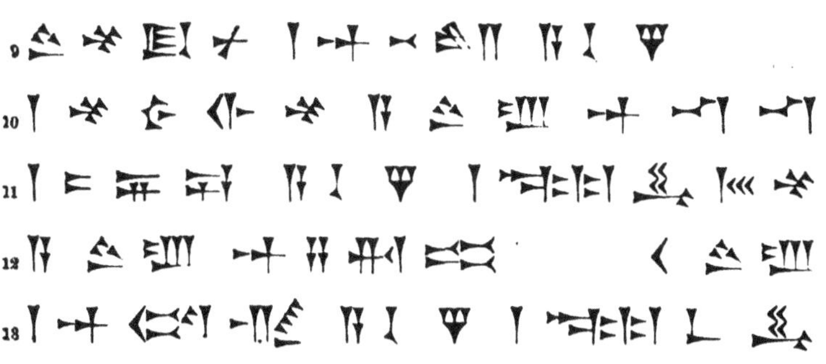

14
15

Left Side.

16

Tablet of a light brown color, 1⅜ x 2 inches. The signs are plainly and neatly made. All the available space on the tablet is used for writing, though the lines and the individual signs are well divided. A large round hole in the middle of line 4, extending into line 5, and a small break at the end of line 7, are the only things that mar the perfection of this little tablet. The words "King of Babylon" are found in the middle of the left side.

Transliteration.	*Translation.*
1 1/3 (mana) 4 ṭu kaspi ša Iddin-Ma duk apal-šu ša	1 ⅓ mana 4 shekels of money which Iddinmarduk, the son of
2 Iḳi-ša-apla apal Nûr-Sin ina ili	2 Ikishâpla, the son of Nûrsin, from
3 A-ra-bi amilu gal-la Iddin-Marduk	3 Arabi, the slave of Iddinmarduk,
4 apal Nûr-Sin iṭ-ṭi-ru i-na(!) araḫ Ululu	4 the son of Nûrsin, will receive in the month Ululu,
5 ša šattu 8 kam Nabû-na'id šar Babili	5 of the 8 th year of Nabûna'id, King of Babylon.
6 ša ûmu ina ili-šu i-rab-bi	6 Every day against him it will increase.
7 kaspu ša a-na manzasa u-da-nu-tu ...	7 The money, which for witness (fees) was given, (Arabi)
8 iddin-nu	8 has given.
9 amilu mu-kin-nu Bil-ḫarran apal-šu ša	9 Witnesses: Belharran, the son of
10 Mu-sal-lim-mu apal amilu šangu Na-na	10 Musallim, the son of the priest of Nana;
11 Tab-ni-i apal-šu ša Nabû-aḫi-iddin	11 Tabnê, the son of Nabûahiddin,
12 apal amilu šangu ilu Za-ri-ḳu u amilu dupsar	12 the son of the priest of Zariku; and the scribe
13 Marduk-musallim apal-šu ša Nabû-šip-uṣur	13 Mardukmusallim, the son of Nabûship-usur,
14 apal Aḫa-ba-ni Babilu araḫ Ululu	14 the son of Ahabâni. Babylon, in the month Ululu,
15 ûmu 28 kam šattu 8 kam Nabû-na'id	15 on the 28 th day, in the 8 th year of Nabûna'id,
16 šar Babili	16 King of Babylon.

NOTES.

1. The word **mana** is omitted. — 2. The scribe had written the sign for **i** first, in place of **Nûr**, and then had changed the former to the latter sign. — 3. **Arabi**, I would take as first having denoted the nationality of the slave, (for he is distinctly called **amilu gal-lu** here,) then the word became a proper name, and we find one **Arabi**, the son of **Bilšunu**, the son of the priest of **Šamaš**, mentioned in Strass., Cambyses 257, 14. 15. (See also note to **Isaggilai**, 26, 6.) Between lines 3 and 4 **apal-šu ša Iḳi-ša-apla**, his father's name, is omitted, and only the family name is given. This is the reason why we find simply **apal** beginning line 4. His father's name is given in line 2, and the scribe evidently thought it unnecessary to repeat. — 4. **iṭ-ṭi-ru**. Half of the sign **iṭ**, and also half of the **ṭi**, is broken off. No traces are visible. The sign for **ša** must evidently be a mistake for **na**; and as both signs are very common, the scribe might have written the one for the other. — 7. **u-da-nu-tu**. A curious form from **nadânu**. For forms with final **tu(m)**, see Strass., Nbk. 78, 4; Nabn. 357; 525, 23; &c.; and for preformative **u**, see Strass., Cyr. 26, 9; 170, 7; 237, 12. — 10. **Mu-sal-lim-mu**. The final syllable must be read **mu** and not **šumu**, as an examination of the same name in 25, 7 will show. **ilu Na-na**. See Z. A. III, p. 5; VII, p. 142; Jensen, Kosmologie p. 102; Sayce, Babylonian Religion pp. 260, 282. Compare also Payne Smith, Thesaurus col. 2387; Hoffmann, Auszüge aus syrischen Akten persischer Märtyrer pp. 130. 151 ff; Lagarde, Agathangelus 1887 p. 135; on Sassanide coins, BOR I, p. 106; ZDMG, 44, 669. — 13. **ilu Za-ri-ḳu**. This god's name is found also in Strass., Cyr. 141, 14; 149, 12; see also 25, 13 of this book. Strassmaier, Verh. des 5ten Intern. Orient. Cong. zu Berlin 1881, B. 42, 22 (p. 134), gives **Za-ar-ri-ḳu** as the name of a man, taken undoubtedly from the name of the god. — 13. **Nabû-šip-uṣur** for **Nabû-šipâ-uṣur**, "may Nebo protect the feet." — 15. Dated in the year 547 B. C.

Iddinmarduk lent his slave Arabi 24 shekels of money in the month Ululu, which the latter was to return in the same month. As a slave was not held responsible for his actions, but his master, the latter, it would seem, did not wish to risk his money for a longer period. Every single day was to increase the amount; at what rate of interest, we do not know. This daily increase seems especially severe, for a slave could not have been but a poor man. The latter was also required, as an additional curb to his business ambition, to pay the witness fees. With this imposition he seems to have cheerfully complied, according to line 8. After all the payments to be made, and considering the short time that the loan had to run, Arabi must have had to contend with great financial embarrassments. Happy he, if he returned the money at the proper time!

NO. 18.

FRONT.

BACK.

Tablet of a grayish brown color, 1⅜ x 1⅜ inches. The writing is good and the signs are plainly made; with the exception of the last five signs of line 8. These are written so closely together and are so lightly made, that it is difficult to decipher them. On the lower edge are two rows of finger nail impressions, each containing sixteen marks. The lower row, however, is more deeply pressed in.

Transliteration.	*Translation.*
1 9 ṭu kaspi Iddin-Marduk apal-šu ša	1 9 shekels of money Iddinmarduk, the son of

2 Iḳî-ša-apla apal Nû.-sin ina ḳâtâ	**2 Ikishapla, the son of Nûrsin, from the hands of**
3 Pu-na-ni-tum a-di ti-lit-tum ši-na	**3 Punanitum, together with double the amount(?)**
4 ša ultu ili mi-ḫir-tu	**4 which, in behalf**
5 ša Ab-la-da na-da-nu aššat-šu	**5 of Ablada, he gave to his wife**
6 ina ḫubulli kaspa-šu maḫ-ḫir	**6 at interest: his money he has received.**
7 ina manzazi ša Tab-ni-i-a	**7 In the presence of Tabnêa,**
8 apal-šu ša Nabû-aḫi-iddin	**8 the son of Nabûahiddin,**
9 apal amilu šangu Ša-maš Nabû-is-kip	**9 the son of the priest of Shamash; Nabûiskip,**
10 apal-šu ša Marduk-šum-ibni apal Idanin-Nabû	**10 the son of Mardukshumibni, the son of Idaninnabû.**
11 Barsiba araḫ Adaru ûmu 12 kam	**11 Barsiba, in the month Adar, on the 12th day,**
12 šattu 8 kam Nabû-na'id šar Babili	**12 in the 8th year of Nabûna'id, King of Babylon.**
13 daḫ-ḫu-tum lâ ba-ši-i	**13 A further demand there is not.**

NOTES.

3. **ti-lit-tum.** The meaning of this word is doubtful. Peiser, Bab. Ver. p. 309, translates "Auflage"; and Tallqvist, p. 41, follows him. The word occurs also in the same form in Strass., Nabn. 1058, 8. **ši-na** really means "two," but if it must be translated thus, it ought to precede its substantive. — 4. **mi-ḫir-tu** is used as a preposition and means "opposite." Notice the identity of the signs **ḫir** and **tu**. — 5. **na-ta-nu** must be read **na-da-nu**. See Deluge Tablets, l. 187, tu-ud-*da*-a at-ta "thou shalt know." — 7. **manzazi.** For other examples see Talq. p. 103, and Peiser, Bab. Ver. LIII, 6. The word in the Deluge Tablets, lines 141 and 143, means "a resting place" (Haupt, B. A. I. 173). — 9. The name of the god Shamash is here spelled out, usually the ideogram **tu** is written. — **Barsiba** or "Borsippa," the name of the Babylonian city founded by Nebuchadrezar. Many tablets are dated from this city. See Strass., Cyr., Inhaltsverz. p. 14; Camb., Inhaltsverz. p. 16; &c. — 12. Hence in the year 547 B. C. — 13. The meaning of **daḫ-ḫu-tum** is uncertain. I would connect it with **daḫû** "to touch," and **diḫu** "neighborhood." Its position at the end of the tablet, and the fact that it is used in the phrase in which **rašûtu** is generally used, would give it a meaning similar to "demand."

The sense I derive from the tablet is this: Iddinmarduk has lent Ablada 9 shekels of money, together with a small amount that he gave to the latter's wife. He now receives his money back. The interest on the 9 shekels and on the amount loaned besides, has now become as great as the latter amount. Hence we have the expression *double* amount. The entire sense of the tablet rests upon the supposition that "*telittum*" means "*amount*."

NO. 19.

FRONT.

BACK.

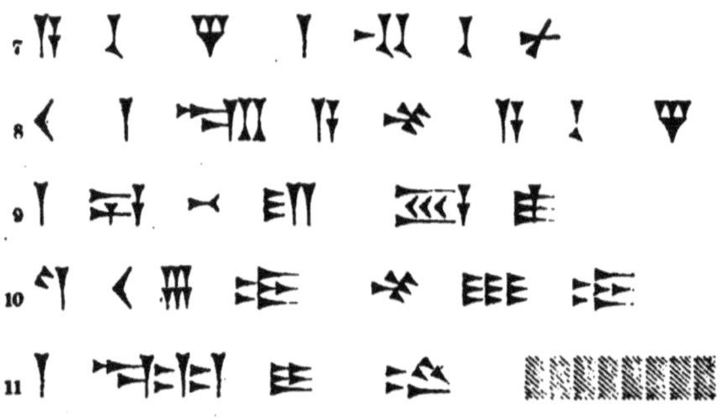

Tablet of a light brown color, 1¼ x 1⅝ inches. The signs are crudely made and much of the space is not used. The lower right hand corner of the reverse is effaced, destroying the word *Babili*, traces of the upper part of which, however, can yet be clearly distinguished. Two rows of finger nail marks are found on the upper side: the first with eight, and the second with thirteen indentations. Undoubtedly the first row also contained thirteen marks, and five of these have been broken off.

Transliteration.

1 1/3 ma-na 4 ṭu kaspi ḫubullu

2 kaspi-šu ša 2 ta šanâti

3 Iddinmarduk ina ḳâtâ

4 Ba-la-ṭu ma-ḫi-ir

Translation.

1 ⅓ mana 4 shekels of money, the interest

2 on his money for two years,

3 Iddinmarduk from the hands of

4 Balatu has received(?).

5 ina mansazi ša	5 In the presence of
6 Bil-aḫi-iḳi-ša	6 Belahikisha,
7 apal-šu ša Bil-šu-nu	7 the son of Belshunu;
8 u Bil-apal-iddin apal-šu ša	8 and Belapaliddin, the son of
9 Ĭ-mid-su araḫ Šabaṭu	9 Emidsu. In the month Shabat,
10 ûmu 16 kam šattu 9 kam	10 on the 16th day, in the 9th year of
11 Nabû-na'id šar [mat Babili].	11 Nabûna'id, King of Babylon.

NOTES.

4. ma-ḫi-ir. The sign for ḫi is blurred and indistinct, and I was led to read u in its stead in the first edition of this book. Now, indeed, the form of the word is clear and the sense of the passage is obvious. The same form occurs in 30, 8. — 5. mansazi. Consult note to 18, 7. — 9. As no mention of a city is made, we are led to infer that Babylon is meant. — 10. This tablet is therefore dated in the year 546 B. C.

Balatu has loaned a certain sum of money from Iddinmarduk and now, at end of two years, he brings the interest, ⅓ mana and 4 shekels. Or, as a mana contains 60 shekels, he brings 24 shekels. We are not told the rate of interest in this case; and as the latter varied greatly from exorbitant to insignificant rates, we are entirely in the dark, how much the sum of money loaned amounted to.

NO. 20.

FRONT.

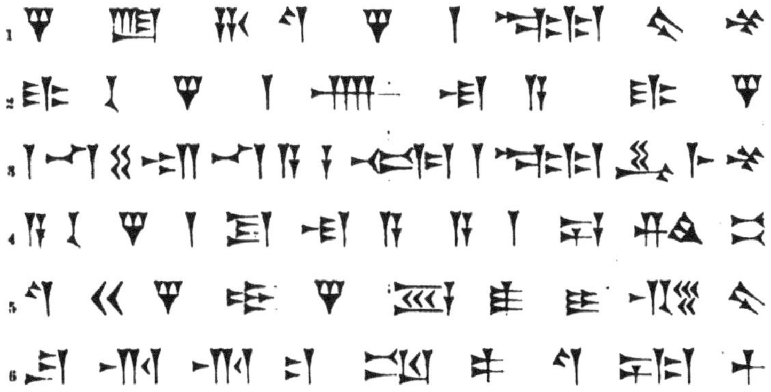

BACK.

Tablet of a light gray color. 1⅓ x 1¾ inches. The signs are very indistinct, as if made by a dull stylus. The left edge is not inscribed, otherwise all the available space is used. The only serious imperfection is a small round hole in line 11 of the reverse, breaking out the signs for *Bani-ia*. A few other unimportant lacunae occur in lines 14 and 15.

Transliteration.	*Translation.*
1 4 ṭu kaspi ša Nabû-balaṭ-iddin	1 4 shekels of money of Nabûbalatiddin,
2 mâr-šu ša Ṣil-la-a mâr ša	2 the son of Sillâ, the son of
3 Na-ši-ir-na-a ša ina ili Nabû-aḫi-iddin	3 Nashèrnâ, which he is to receive from Nabûahiddin,
4 apal-šu ša Šu-la-a apal Î-gi-bi	4 the son of Shulâ, the son of Egibi.
5 ûmu 24 kam ša araḫ Šabaṭu i-nam-din	5 On the 24 th day of the month Shabat he will give
6 pa-ri-ri-is al-pa siparra	6 the sheep(?), the ox, (and) the copper,
7 ša Mu-ši-zib-Bil a-na	7 which Mushezibbel to
8 Nabû-aḫi-iddin id-di-nu	8 Nabûahiddin gave.
9 amilu mu-kin-nu Nabû-iddin apal-šu ša	9 Witnesses: Nabûiddin, the son of
10 Mu-ši-zib-Bil apal Na-ši-i-Nabû-apla	10 Mushezibbel, the son of Nashènabûapla;

11 Iddin-Nabû apal-šu ša [Bani-ia] apal Du-ub-bi	11 Iddinnabû, the son of Bania, the son of Dûbbi;
12 u amilu dupsar Nabû-aḫi-iddin apal-šu ša	12 and the scribe Nabûahiddin, the son of
13 Šu-la-a apal Ì-gi-bi Babilu	13 Shulâ, the son of Egibi. Babylon,
14 arah Šabaṭu ûmu 23(?) kam šattu 9 kam	14 in the month Shabat, on the 23rd day, in the 9th year of
15 Nabû-na'id šar Babili.	15 Nabûna'id, King of Babylon.

NOTES.

2. mâru and aplu are used indiscriminately in the Contract Tablets. — 8. The sign for ša is a little peculiar. We generally find *two* small vertical wedges above one heavy vertical wedge, here we have only *one*. I have printed three in other cases, because my type did not contain the sign with two, and because it is more easily recognized. — 6. pa-ri-ri-is I would connect with parratu "a female sheep" (Tallqvist, p. 117; Delitzsch, Assyr. Stud. p. 166). The word, however, if read correctly, must be classed among the unknown. — 11. Without doubt Bani-ia, as the first signs show. There is room for only two signs. — 13. The form of gi is curious. The other parts of the sign the scribe must have forgotten, as such a sign was not in use among the Babylonians. On tablet 30, lines 2 and 3, of this book, we find it written in the form of a single vertical wedge. The size of the break in this line will admit of but two more vertical wedges. — 14. Tablet dated in the year 546 B. C., as the preceding.

Nabubalatiddin has lent Nabuahiddin 4 shekels of money. The latter being unable to pay, agrees to give instead of cash payment the sheep, the ox, and the copper utensils just given to him by Mushezibbel, one of his debtors. *Alpu* is the general name for cattle ; he therefore might have promised a calf or a cow.

NO. 21.

FRONT.

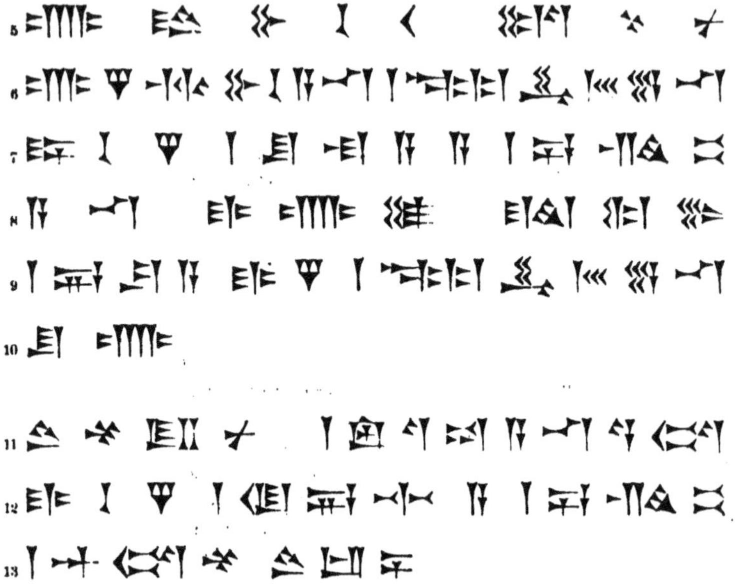

BACK.

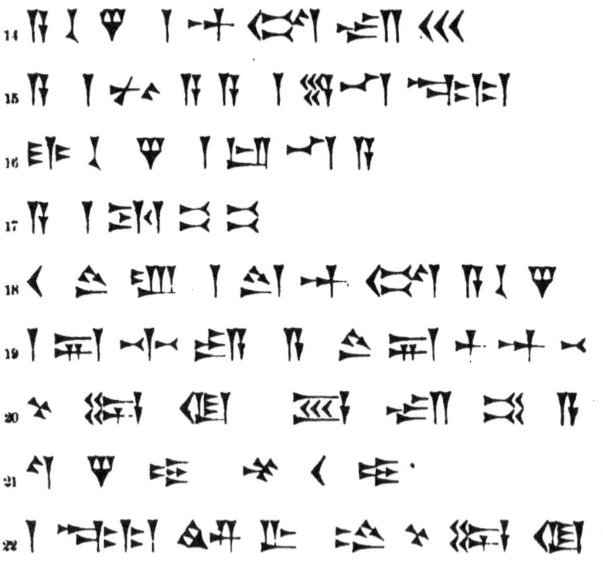

Tablet of a dark yellow color, shading to black at the lower right hand corner of the obverse. Size: 2 x 2¾ inches. At the end of the tablet there is a considerable space (¼ inch) not used. Also between lines 10 and 11, the scribe has left a large space. None of the four edges are written upon. The upper edge of the obverse is broken off at the two corners, the larger break being on the right side. The extreme right of the obverse is also damaged in many places. The signs are large and beautifully made; and the lines are well spaced.

Transliteration.	*Translation.*
1 . . . . šum-ukin-na mâr-šu ša Iddin-	1 . . . . . shumukinna, the son of Iddin . . . .
2 ina ḫu-ud lib-bi-šu Kal-ba-a mâr-šu	2 in the pleasure of his heart, Kalbâ, the son of
3 [ša] Ia-ḫa-ta ša Nabû-aḫi-iddin-na [mâ -šu]	3 Iahata, — whom Nabûahiddinna, the son of
4 ša Nabû-aḫi-iddin-na ul-tu ṣi-ḫi-ri	4 Nabûahiddinna, from smallness
5 u-rab-bu-šu u li-nad-nu	5 had made him great, and had indeed given
6 u ša iḳ-bu-šu a-na Nabû-aḫi-iddin-na	6 also what he had promised him, — to Nabûahiddinna,
7 mâr-šu ša Šu-la-a apal Î-gi-bi	7 the son of Shulâ, the son of Egibi,
8 a-na mâru-u-tu id-di-in	8 for adoption gave.
9 Kal-ba-a mâr ša Nabû-aḫi-iddin-na	9 Kalbâ, the son of Nabûahiddinna,
10 šu-u	10 is he.
11 amilu mu-kin-nu Lu-uṣ-a-na-nûri-Marduk	11 Witnesses: Lûsananûrimarduk,
12 mâr-šu ša Ki-rib-ti apal Î-gi-bi	12 the son of Kiribti, the son of Egibi;
13 Marduk-iddin amilu IB-bani	13 Mardukiddin, the carpenter,
14 apal-šu ša Marduk-ipi-iš	14 the son of Mardukepêsh,
15 apal Zir-ai Iddin-na-Nabû	15 the son of Zirai; Iddinnanabû,
16 mâr-šu ša It-na-a	16 the son of Ibnâ,
17 apal Da-bi-bi	17 the son of Dabibi;
18 u amilu dupsar Arad-Marduk apal-šu ša	18 and the scribe Aradmarduk, the son of
19 Bit-ti-ia apal amilu i-maš Bil	19 Bittia, the son of the priest of Bel.
20 Babilu araḫ Samna-am-a	20 Babylon, in the month Marcheshwan,
21 ûmu 4 kam šattu 10 kam	21 on the 4th day, in the 10th year of
22 Nabû-na'id šar Babili.	22 Nabûna'id, King of Babylon.

NOTES.

1. The name does not occur again on the tablet; we therefore cannot supply the missing links. — 3. That the son bears the same name as his father is very rare. The break at the end of the line will admit of only the two signs **apal** and **šu**. — 4. 5. "From smallness had made him great" is an expression for which I can find no parallel in any

contract tablet. The sense, however, is very plain. Kalbâ had been a slave, and Nabûahiddin adopted him, thus making him a free man, and giving him all the privileges that freedom implied. This was, indeed, a leap from smallness to greatness. — 5. li-nad-nu with the precative li. This occurs often. — 6. This Nabûahiddin must be the father, the one mentioned in line 4. — 8. mâ.ûtu is the term regularly used to signify "adoption." — 9. 10. These lines give the gist of the whole tablet. It is a quaint sentence and is entirely to the point. — 13. ID-bani "carpenter," a provisional translation. — 19. i-maš is an ideogram. The name of this scribe occurs also in 25, 17. But here his family name is given as **apal amilu šangu Bil**, thus proving conclusively that i-maš is a synonym of šangu, and possibly ought to be read šangu. For other passages where it occurs, see Tallq. p. 45. — 20. It is curious to note how the name of the month Marcheshwan is spelled out. The first of the three signs is deemed sufficient in nearly all the other cases where the name occurs. Cf. 15, 14; 27, 4. 5. — 21. Dated in the year 545 B. C.

Nabuahiddin had become possessed of Kalba, the slave of Nabu(?)-shumukin. He himself had no issue, and was thus led to adopt the slave, to whom he had undoubtedly taken a fancy. In order to do so, he had to obtain the consent of Kalba's former master, so that no stain might remain upon his character or his social standing. This course would also effectually prevent all legal proceedings for reclaiming the slave on the ground that he belonged to the king, that he had never been properly sold, or for any other real or fictitious reason.

It was a common custom among the ancient Babylonians, if they were childless, to adopt worthy slaves. And if we remember that many noble and educated men of neighboring nations were reduced to slavery by the frequent and merciless raids of the Babylonian kings, and were brought to Babylon for sale, we shall not at all be surprised to find these taken into Babylonian families and there adopted.

NO. 22.

FRONT.

BACK.

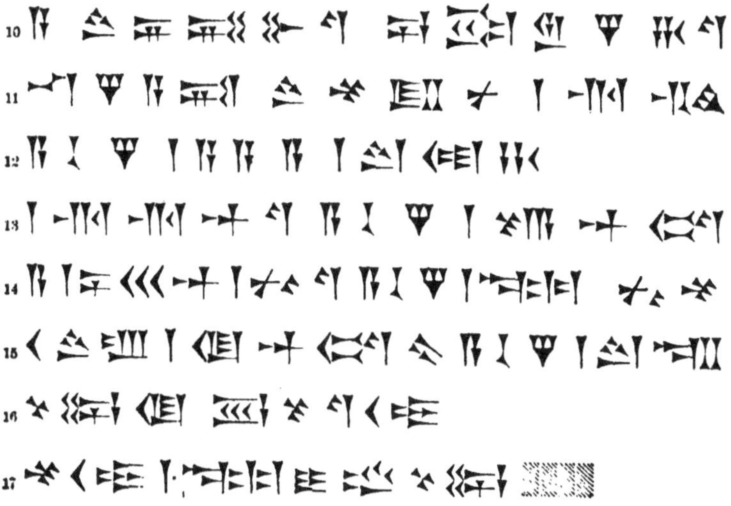

Tablet of a grayish brown color, 1⅜ x 2¾ inches. The upper right hand corner of the obverse is broken off, destroying the end of the first two lines, and also the last sign of the last line of the reverse. All the signs, however, can be easily supplied. The writing is clear, and the signs distinct and well-made. The left side alone bears no inscription.

Transliteration.	*Translation.*
1 1/3 ma-na 5 ṭu kaspi ša [Itti-Marduk-balaṭu]	1 ⅓ mana 5 shekels of money which Itti-mardukbalatu,
2 apal-šu ša Nabû-aḫi-iddin apal Ì-[gi-bi]	2 the son of Nabûahiddin, the son of Egibi,
3 ina ili Arad-Marduk apal-šu ša Marduk-iṭi-ir	3 is to receive from Aradmarduk, the son of Marduketer,

4 apal amilu ša ṭâbti-šu ina araḫ Airu kaspa.a.an	4 the son of the governor of his portion. In the month Air in cash
5 1/3 ma-na 5 ṭu u ḫubulla-šu i-nam-din	5 the ⅓ mana 5 shekels and its interest he will give.
6 Mi-ṣa-tum gal-lat-su maš-ka-nu	6 Misatum, his slave, is the security
7 ša Itti-Marduk-balaṭu a-di ili ša Itti-Marduk-balaṭu	7 of Ittimardukbalatu until that Ittimardukbalatu
8 kaspa-šu i-šal-li-mu Nabû-u-šu-da-kâtâ	8 his money has received. Nabûshudakâtâ,
9 marat-su ša Ta-kiš-Gu-la	9 the daughter of Takishgula,
10 apal amilu ķipu pu-ut i-ṭi-ru ša kaspi	10 the son of the guardian, has received a receipt for the money
11 na-ša-a-ta amilu mu-kin-nu Ri-mut	11 she brought. Witnesses: Rimut,
12 apal-šu ša Ai apal Arad-Nirgal	12 the son of Ai, the son of Aradnergal;
13 Ri-dal-Šamaš apal-šu ša Iṭi -Marduk	13 Ridalshamash, the son of Etêrmarduk,
14 apal Ipi-iš-ilu Zir-ûtu apal-šu ša Nabû-zir-iddin	14 the son of Epêshilu; Zirûtu, the son of Nabûziriddin;
15 u amilu dupsar Itti-Marduk-balaṭu apal-šu ša Arad-Bil	15 and the scribe Ittimardukbalatu, the son of Aradbel.
16 Babilu araḫ Adaru ûmu 10 kam	16 Babylon, in the month Adar, on the 10th day,
17 šattu 10 kam Nabû-na'id šar Babili	17 in the 10th year of Nabûna'id, King of Babylon.

NOTES.

This tablet has already been published by Strassmaier in his autograph texts of the reign of Nabonidus, No. 479. Several of the signs on this tablet are blurred, which fact accounts for the differing readings of the first edition of this book. — 4. amilu ša ṭâbti-šu. See Tallq. p. 76 for other instances. — 5. "its" interest, that is, the interest on the ⅓ mana 5 shekels. — 8. Strassmaier reads Nabû-šip-tum-..., which, in my judgment, is not borne out by the signs on the tablet; the above reading seems to me to be the most likely. — 10. amilu ķipu. Tallqvist on p. 122 gives a number of meanings for this word, and many passages where it occurs. naššta, lit. "brought," then, "lent." — 13. Ri-dal-Šamaš. Strassmaier writes mut in place of dal. But the sign dal is so plainly made, that it can not possibly be mistaken for mut. — 17. Dated 545 B. C.

Ittimardukbalatu has lent Aradmarduk 25 shekels which the latter promises to return with interest during the month Airu (May). Until this payment is made, Ittimardukbalatu retains a female slave of Aradmardukbalatu as security. Nabushudakata is also to receive back the money she loaned, evidently, to Aradmarduk. The former, because she is mentioned on this tablet together with Ittimardukbalatu, and bears the same relation with him to Aradmarduk, she must in some way be connected with the latter. Perhaps she is his wife, though no statement on that point is made.

NO. 23.

FRONT.

BACK.

LEFT SIDE.

15
16

Tablet of a brown color. 1¼ x 2 inches. The signs are plainly written, excepting the name in the first line. It seems as if something had been broken off in the beginning of line 16. As the sense is complete, however, the part effaced may not have contained any writing.

Transliteration.	*Translation.*
1 1/2 ma-na kaspi ša Nabû-rimu-lip-tum	1 ½ mana of money which Nabûremuliptum,
2 mâr-šu ša Šu-zu-bu	2 the son of Shuzubu,
3 amilu rab.ka-a-ri ša šarri	3 the *rabkari* of the king,
4 ina ili Nabû-aḫi-iddin	4 is to receive from Nabûahiddin,
5 amilu dainu mâr-šu ša Šu-la-a	5 the judge, the son of Shulâ,
6 apal Î-gi-bi ina araḫ Adaru	6 the son of Egibi; in the month Adar
7 i-nam-din	7 he will give (it).
8 amilu mu-kin-nu Šu-la-a	8 Witnesses: Shulâ,
9 mâr-šu ša Iḳi-ša-apla apal Iddin-Bil	9 the son of Ikîshapla, the son of Iddinbel;
10 Iddin-Marduk apal-šu ša Bil-šum-išku-un	10 Iddinmarduk, the son of Belshumishkun,
11 apal amilu ḳipu Na-din dup-sar	11 the son of the guardian; Nadin the scribe,
12 mâr amilu IR.ŠAL.TAB(P .ŠA Babilu	12 son of the .... Babylon,
13 araḫ Šabaṭu ûmu 2 kam šattu 11 kam	13 in the month Shabat, on the 2nd day, in the 11 th year of
14 Nabû-na'id šar Babili	14 Nabûna'id, King of Babylon.
15 ri-ḫi-it 2 1/2 ma-na kaspi	15 The remainder 2½ mana of money
16 ...... lâ i-ša šarri	16 . .... does not belong to the king.

NOTES.

3. amilu rab.ka-a-ri. This was the official appointed by the government to see that the weights and measures of the merchants were of correct legal size. **kâru** means a dry measure; it is the כר of I Kings iv: 22. In Ezek. xlv: 11 it is also used as a liquid measure. For other instances where this official is mentioned see Tallq. p. 79. — 4. This Nabûahiddin is mentioned also in 12, 7. 9. 15. — 11. amilu ḳipu: cf. 15, 10 and note. **dupsar.**

This form is rarely found on the contract tablets. amilu is omitted at the beginning, and **sar** is added. Ordinarily the sign for **dup** suffices for the word **dupsar**; cf. 11, 17; 12, 19; 13, 16; 14, 24; &c. — 12. The reading of the title of the father of the scribe is very uncertain. amilu **IR** occurs very often on the tablets (Tallq. p. 50), but the remaining signs are so indistinct, that I venture to give them only with great reserve. — 13. In the year 544 B. C. — 15. The whole debt must have consisted of 3 mana, only ½ mana of which was to be paid in the month Adar; about this remainder there was undoubtedly another tablet in existence.

Naburemuliptum has loaned Nabuahiddin ½ mana, which the latter promises to pay back in the month Adar (March). Naburemuliptum must have belonged to the household of the king, and the ½ mana must have been loaned from the king's funds; for, in lines 15 and 16, we find a remainder mentioned which did not belong to the king, but was the private property of Naburemuliptum. The fact that there is no statement to the effect that the ½ mana belonged to the king, is no proof; for Naburemuliptum had lent the money, and he alone was responsible for its return. He also, undoubtedly, kept a private account of his loans and disbursements for the king. The attributes in lines 3, 5, 11, and possibly 12, show that the contracting parties must have been of high standing, and render the above explanation of the tablet very probable.

NO. 24.

FRONT.

BACK.

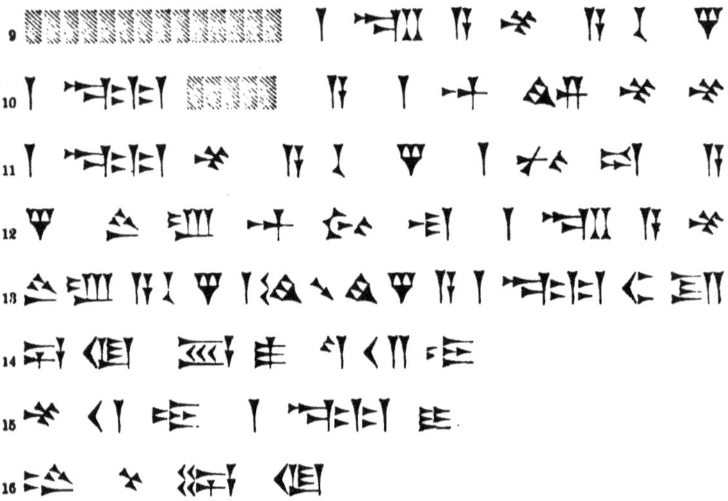

Tablet of a dark gray color, 1⅜ x 2⅜ inches. On the left side there is no writing. A few lines of both obverse and reverse are prolonged over the right side. The writing is plain throughout. Some portions of the left side of the obverse are covered with a hard substance, which renders a few of the signs difficult to read. In lines 5 and 8 in the lacunæ, traces of the signs for "hubullu" can be seen. But on the left upper corner nothing can be read, as the tablet is there covered with this flinty accumulation, the removal of which would, I fear, entail the partial destruction of the tablet.

Transliteration.	*Translation.*
1 3 ma-na kaspi ša Iddin-Marduk apal-šu ša	1 3 mana of money which Iddinmarduk, the son of
2 Iḳi-ša-apla apal Nûr-sin ina ili	2 Ikishapla, the son of Nûrsin, is to receive from
3 Nabû-ban-aḫa apal-šu ša Iḳi-ša-apla apal Na-din-Marduk	3 Nabûbanaha, the son of Ikishapla, the son of Nadinmarduk.
4 ša arḫa ina ili 1 ma-ni-i 1 ṭu kaspi	4 Every month (at the rate of) upon one mana 1 shekel of money
5 ina [ḫubulli] i-rab-bi Bil-ri-man-ni	5 at interest shall increase. Belrimanni,
6 apal-šu ša Marduk-nusallim pu-uš	6 the son of Mardukmusallim, a receipt
7 i-ti-ru na-din arḫa-ta.a.an	7 has received (and) has given. Every month
8 [ḫubulla] i-nam-din	8 interest he will give.

9 [amilu mu-kin-nu] **Bil-apal-iddin apal-šu ša**	9 Witnesses: Belapaliddin, the son of
10 **Nabû-[iddin(?)] apal Rammân-šum-iddin**	10 Nabûiddin, the son of Rammânshum-iddin;
11 **Nabû-iddin apal-šu ša Zir-ukin apal**	11 Nabûiddin, the son of Zirukin, the son
12 **ša** amilu **šangu Gula Bil-apal-iddin**	12 of the priest of Gula; Belapaliddin,
13 amilu **dupsar apal-šu ša Daḫ-ḫi-ša(?) apal Nabû-lit-su**	13 the scribe, the son of Dahhisha, the son of Nabûlitsu.
14 **Babilu araḫ Šabaṭu ûmu 12 kam**	14 Babylon, in the month Shabat, on the 12 th day,
15 **šattu 11 kam Nabû-na'id**	15 in the 11 th year of Nabûna'id,
16 **šar Babili**	16 King of Babylon.

NOTES.

3. **Nabû-ban-aḫa.** Peiser in his Babyl. Ver. wrongly transcribes this name **Nabû-ban-zir.** The last sign never has the meaning : **ziru** "seed." Strass. in his Camby. correctly transcribes **Nabû-ban-aḫu** (2, 13; 309, 11; 388, 17). — 4. The rate would therefore be 12 shekels a year on one mana, or 20 per cent. The form **ma-ni-i** is generally used in this connection. For other examples see Tallq. p. 96 and Peiser Babyl. Ver. p. 319*b*. — 9. amilu **mu-kin-nu** is evidently demanded by the sense. — 10. **Nabû-iddin.** Traces of the iddin can be distinctly seen. — 11. The **šu** at the end of the line is either omitted or written so lightly as to escape detection. — 13. **Daḫ-ḫi-ša.** I doubt whether this name is read correctly.

Iddinmarduk had loaned Nabubanaha 3 mana through the agency of Belrimanni. This money was to bear interest monthly, and consequently monthly payments are demanded. Belrimanni seems to have been a man like the modern real estate agent. He gives a receipt for the money intrusted to him to Iddinmarduk, and receives one from Nabubanaha, to whom he had given the money; here his responsibility ends. He doubtless received a commission commensurate with the service he had performed for Iddinmarduk from the latter. This we might find recorded upon another tablet.

NO. 25.

FRONT.

1 

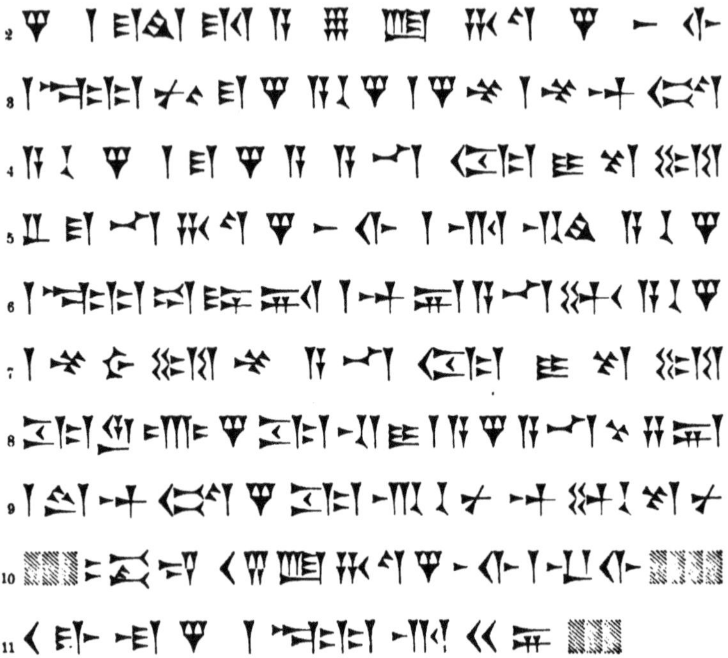

BACK.

20 21 22

Tablet of a dark gray color, 2 x 2¾ inches. The left side is smooth and flat, and contains no writing. In general, the writing upon the tablet is plain, only in some places it is worn away to such a degree that decipherment is impossible. The upper left hand corner of the obverse, as well as of the reverse, is entirely broken off. At the end of the tablet there is also a bad break, but this probably contained only a few signs. Line 11 is just on the lower edge, which it completely fills.

Transliteration.	*Translation.*
1 **11 ṭu kaspi ša ina pân .... [apal-šu]**	1 11 shekels of money which are to be received from ......, the son
2 **ša Id-da-a 9 ṭu kaspi ša ina pân**	2 of Iddâ, (and) 9 shekels of money which are to be received from
3 **Nabû-zir-iḳî-ša apal-šu ša Šakan-šum Iddin-Marduk**	3 Nabûzirikîsha, the son of Shakanshum, — Iddinmarduk,
4 **apal-šu ša Iḳî-ša-apla a-na ili i-ti-li**	4 the son of Ikîshâpla, upon (his) account are made out;
5 **1/3 ma-na kaspi ša ina pân Ri-mut apal-šu ša**	5 ⅓ mana of money, which is to be received from Rimut, the son of
6 **Nabû-ukin-apla Î-a-na-ṣir apal-šu ša**	6 Nabûkinapla, — Eanasir, the son of
7 **Mu-sal-li-mu a-na i-li i-ti-li**	7 Musallim, upon (his) account is made out;
8 **ka-ru-u ša ka-pak-i A-ša-a-na-šad ṣa-bit**	8 a measure of ...... Ashânashad took;
9 **Arad-Marduk ša ka-ri-šu-nu an-us-ti-nu**	9 Aradmarduk according to their measures ......
10 ... **ṣiri 15 ṭu kaspi ša ina pân Rad-ši-......**	10 ...... of land; 15 shekels which are to be received from Radshi ......
11 **u gal-la ša Nabû-ri-man-ni ......**	11 and the slave of Nabûrimanni ...... (and)
12 **5 ṭu kaspi ša ina pân Tab-ni-i-**	12 5 shekels of money which are to be received from Tabnêa,
13 **apal** amilu **šangu** ilu **Za-ri-ḳu a-ḫa-a-ta-šu-nu**	13 the son of the priest of Zariku, are their shares.
14 amilu **mu-kin-nu Marduk-iṭi-ir apal-šu ša**	14 Witnesses: Marduketêr, the son of

15 **Rimut apal Arad-Nirgal Nabû-iriš**	15 Rimut, the son of Aradnergal; Nabû-eresh,
16 **apal-šu ša Tab-ni-i-a apal Aḫa-ba-ni**	16 the son of Tabnêa, the son of Ahabâni;
17 **u amilu dupsar Arad-Marduk apal-šu ša Bit-ti-ia**	17 and the scribe Aradmarduk, the son of Bittia,
18 **apal amilu šangu Bil Babilu araḫ Dûzu**	18 the son of the priest of Bel. Babylon, in the month Dûzu,
19 **ûmu 24 kam šattu 11 kam Nabû-na'id šar**	19 on the 24th day, in the 11th year of Nabûna'id, King
20 **Babili 10 gur ši.bar ša**	20 of Babylon. 10 measures of grain, which ......
21 **la-pa-ni It-ti-**............ [**apal**(?)]	21 is to receive from Itti......., (the son of)
22 **Bil-naṣir a-na**	22 Belnasir for .... ..

NOTES.

1. **ina pân** is here equivalent to **ina muḫḫi** or, as I prefer to read, **ina ili**. It means "in the service of," and then in an extended sense, "to be received from." See Tallq. p. 115, **pânu**, 3. — 8. A very difficult line. **ka-ru-u** I take to mean "measure," though that word is generally written **kâru** (cf. Tallq. p. 79) and not **karû**. But then the Greek *κόρος* has both vowels short, showing that the pronunciation must have varied. **ka-pak-i** can possibly be some variety of grain, the general term for which, **ši.bar**, the scribe mentions in line 20. — 9. **an-us-ti-nu** can only be a provisional reading. — 10. **ṣi-i**. Aradmarduk must therefore have received his share in real estate. — 13. **a-ḫa-ʾ-ta-šu-nu**. This form is found also in Strass., Nabn. 572, 10; 653, 9; and Nbk. 300, 7. — Dated in the year 544 B. C. — 20. The scribe had forgotten to insert the three lines 20–22 in their proper place in the body of the writing, therefore, in order not to omit them entirely, he adds them as a postscript here at the end. — 21. **la-pa-ni** is the exact equivalent of the Hebrew לִפְנֵי. For other examples see Tallq. pp. 89, 90; Peiser, Bab. Ver. CXXX, 10; S. A. Smith, Keilschrifttexte Assurbanipals III, p. 59; and Del., Assyr. Gram. p. 224.

The explanation of this tablet is easier than its translation. Very likely the tablet has reference to proceedings in some law court. A certain amount of money and grain, perhaps an inheritance, is divided among Iddinmarduk, Eanasir, Ashanashad, Aradmarduk, and finally two other persons, whose names are broken off. Iddinmarduk gets 20 shekels; Eanasir, also 20; Ashanashad, a measure of some substance, the value of which probabably also amounted to 20 shekels; Aradmarduk takes his share *according to their measures*, that is, 20 shekels worth, in real estate; then the first nameless person receives his 20 shekels, 15 from Radshi...... and the slave of Naburimanni, and 5 from Tabnea; finally, Itti ..... pays to the last creditor the latter's 20 shekels in grain.

NO. 26.

FRONT.

BACK.

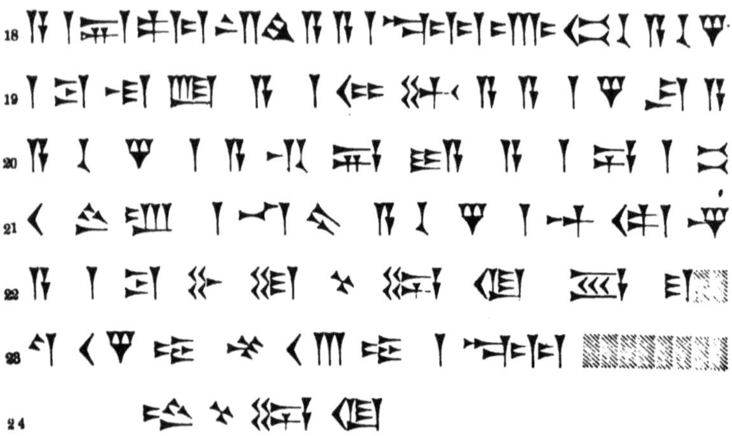

LEFT SIDE.

Tablet of a dar'- amber color shading to black, 1⅝ x 2⅞ inches. The signs are well made, and cover the entire surface of the tablet. Both corners of the right side are broken off, rendering lines 1, 10-15, 22, and 23 incomplete. This tablet undoubtedly belongs to the reign of Nabuna'id, as the break in line 23, though large in extent in the above text, will admit of but one sign on the tablet.

Transliteration.	*Translation.*
1 1/2 ma-na 6 ṭu kaspi ša Itti-Marduk-......-balaṭu	1 ½ mana, 6 shekels of money, which Ittimarduk....balatu,
2 apal-šu ša Nabû-aḫi-iddin apal Î-gi-bi	2 the son of Nabûahiddin, the son of Egibi,
3 ina ili Na-din apal-šu ša Nirgal-iṭir	3 is to receive from Nadin, the son of Nergaletèr,
4 apal Ba-bu-tu u Nu-ub-ta-a aššat-šu	4 the son of Babutu and Nûbtâ, his wife,
5 marat-su ša Nabû-mu-ši-ni-ud-da	5 the daughter of Nabûmushenudda,
6 apal Î-sag-gil-ai ina lib-bi	6 the son of Esaggilai. Thereupon
7 ša 1/3 ma-na 6 ṭu kaspi ša arḫa ina ili	7 ⅓ mana, 6 shekels of money every month at the rate of
8 1 ma-ni-i 1 ṭu kaspi ina ili-šu-nu	8 (upon) 1 mana 1 shekel of money, against them

9 i-"at-bi u 1/4 10 ṭu kaspi u-šib-u	9 are to increase, and ¼ (on every) 10 shekels of money they are to place
10 ša biti šâdi i-di bit-ia	10 in the house to the east hand of my house,
11 u ti-ra kaspi-ia maš-ka-[nu]	11 and they are to return my money. The security
12 ṣab-ta ti-"a-šu ia-[a-tu(?)]	12 they took, they are to return it to me(?).
13 bit-su-nu gab-bi maš-k[a-nu]	13 Their whole house is security,
14 a-di ili ša kaspi-šu i-šu-[u]	14 until that his money is (paid).
15 amilu mu-kin-nu Nabû-mu-ši-ni-ud-[da]	15 Witnesses: Nabûmusheniudda,
16 apal-šu ša Bil-zir-ibni apal Î-sag-gil-ai	16 the son of Belziribni, the son of Esaggilai;
17 Nabû-ga-mil apal-šu ša Nabû-mu-ši-ni-ud-da	17 Nabûgamil, the son of Nabûmusheniudda,
18 apal Î-sag-gil-ai Nabû-uṣur-šu apal-šu ša	18 the son of Esaggilai; Nabûsurshu, the son of
19 Ba-la-ṭu apal Mi-ṣir-ai Iḳi-ša-apla	19 Balatu, the son of Misirai; Ikîshâpla,
20 apal-šu ša A-pak-kal-ia apal Î-gi-bi	20 the son of Appakkalia, the son of Egibi;
21 u amilu dupsar Na-din apal-šu ša Nirgal-iṭir	21 and the scribe Nadin, the son of Nergaletèr,
22 apal Ba-bu-tu Babilu araḫ Nisannu	22 the son of Babûtu. Babylon, in the month Nisan,
23 ûmu 14 kam šattu 13 kam Nabû-na'id	23 on the 14th day, in the 13th year of Nabûna'id,
24 šar Babili	24 King of Babylon.
25 ina a-ša-bi ša Bil-lit-su-nu	25 In the presence of Bellitsunu,
26 ummu ša Na-din	26 the mother of Nadin.

NOTES.

1. There is a break at the end of the line. **Itti-marduk-balaṭu**, however is a complete and common name. (See index to proper names.) There might have been some flaw in the clay of the tablet when the scribe wrote it, and this may have led him to pass over the small space. If this be so, the name is complete. — 6. **Î-sag-gil-ai**. (Cf. also 16, 1. 10, and note.) It is a question whether these names ending in *ai* are adjective forms or have passed over and become ordinary proper names. I should be inclined to the latter view. We have a good parallel in the proper names of slaves among the Romans. "Syrus, Medus" at first meant "the Syrian, the Mede," then the terms became used as ordinary names. In line 19 we have **Mi-ṣir-ai** "the Egyptian" also used as a proper name. Generally, however, these forms are family names. **ina libbi ša** "thereupon." See Peiser's renderings, Bab. Ver. p. 318*b*. — The real interest shall be one shekel on every

mana, that is, 1⅚ per cent. But to this amount must be added the interest spoken of in line 9, which is 2⅓ per cent, making the total interest for every month 4 1-6 per cent. ma-ni-i. See Tallq. p. 96. — 9. u-š.b-u. Strass., Nbk. 137, 11, has the form uš-šib-u. — 11. 12. ti-ra. A peculiar form from târu. It is in the dual, agreeing with the subject: Nadin and his wife. ṣabta is in the dual for the same reason. — 22. The first signs show that "Nisan" is the month mentioned. — 25. 26. Women, as a rule, were not allowed to act as witnesses. We therefore find the short note simply to mention the fact that Nadin's mother, Belitsunu, was also present at the signing of the contract, thus signifying her assent to her son's actions.

Ittimardukbalatu had loaned Nadin and his wife 36 shekels. These were to increase at the fixed rate of 4 1-6 per cent, about the usual percentage for that time. Nadin and Nubta had evidently had some business transaction before with Ittimardukbalatu, for we find a *security* mentioned in line 11; but, on account of the break, we are debarred from learning of what nature this security was. However, they gave this back, and, in addition, they gave their house as security in return for the money loaned.

NO. 27.

FRONT.

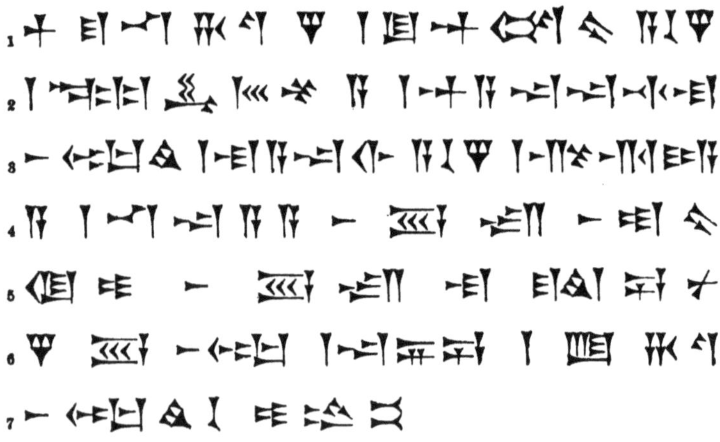

BACK.

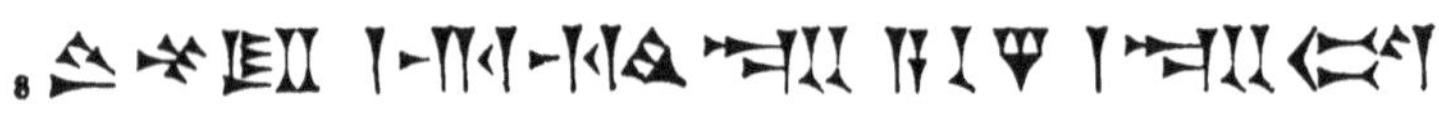

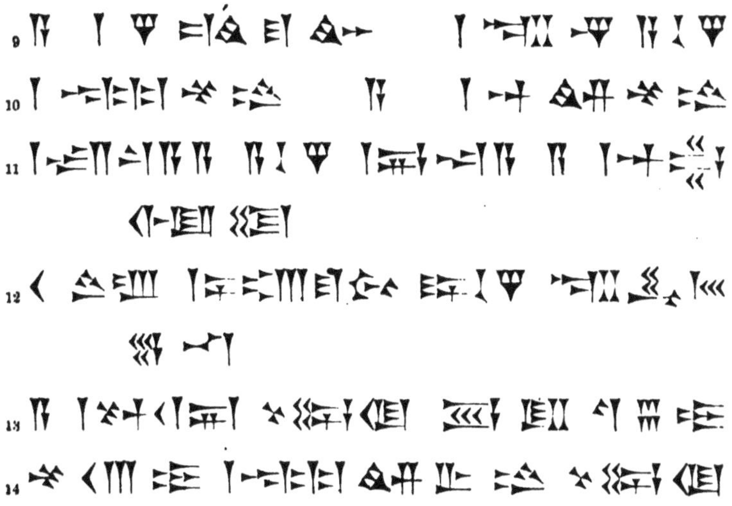

Tablet, on obverse, of a light brown color shading to dark brown; on reverse, from dark brown to almost black. The signs are distinct and prettily made. Size: 1⅝ x 2⅛. The sides are free from writing, excepting the right side, which contains a few signs of lines prolonged from the reverse.

Transliteration.	*Translation.*
1 1/2 ma-na kaspi ša Itti-Marduk-balaṭu apal-šu ša	1 ½ mana of money which Ittimardukbalatu, the son of
2 Nabû-aḫi-iddin apal A-ba-ba-ti-la	2 Nabûahiddin, the son of Ababatila,
3 ina ili La-a-ba-ši apal-šu ša Zi-ri-ia	3 is to receive from Lâbashi, the son of Ziria,
4 apal Na-ba-ai ina araḫ Samna ina-ad-din	4 the son of Nabâ; in the month Marcheshwan, he will give (it).
5 ki-i ina araḫ Samna lâ id-i-nu	5 If in the month Marcheswan he does not give (it),
6 ša arḫa ina ili 1 ma-ni-i 1 ṭu kaspi	6 every month (at the rate of) upon 1 mana 1 shekel of money
7 ina ili-šu i-rab-bi	7 against him it shall increase.
8 amilu mu-kin Ri-mut-Bil apal-šu ša Bil-Marduk	8 Witnesses: Rimutbel, the son of Belmarduk,
9 apal Ša-am-ma-' Bil-iṭir apal-šu ša	9 the son of Shâmma'; Beletêr, the son of
10 Nabû-šum-uṣur apal Rammânu-šum-uṣur	10 Nabûshumusur, the son of Rammânushumusur;
11 Su-ḳa-ai apal-šu ša Kal-ba-a apal Babu-u-tu	11 Sukâ, the son of Kalbâ, the son of Babûtu;

12 u amilu dupsar Bani-um-ma-gu mâr-šu ša Bil-aḫi-iddin-na	12 and the scribe Baniummagu, the son of Belahiddinna,
13 apal Ṣir-diš-bit Babilu araḫ Ululu ûmu 6 kam	13 the son of Sirdishbit. Babylon, in the month Ululu, on the 6th day,
14 šattu 13 kam Nabû-na'id šar Babili	14 in the 13th year of Nabûna'id, King of Babylon.

NOTES.

4. ina-ad-din. The word spelled in this way occurs also in Strass. Nabn. 282, 7. — 6. Rate of interest for every month 1⅔ per cent, or for the year 20 per cent. — 8. mu-kin. The final nu might have been omitted by the scribe by mistake. The form, however, occurs again in Strass. Nabn. 153, 5; Peiser, Bab. Ver. CXLVII, 10. — Ša-am-ma-'. A shortened form for Šama-ilu (Strass., Verzeich. zu den Liverpool Insch. p. 60.) — 14. Dated in the year 542 B. C., as the preceding tablet.

Ittimardukbalatu has loaned Labashi half of a mana, and has made an agreement with him that the money is to be returned during the month Marcheshwan. Until that time the money shall bear no interest. But, if payment is not made during that month, then interest at 20 per cent a year will accrue against him. Hence the money is really loaned for an indefinite period of years.

NO. 28.

FRONT.

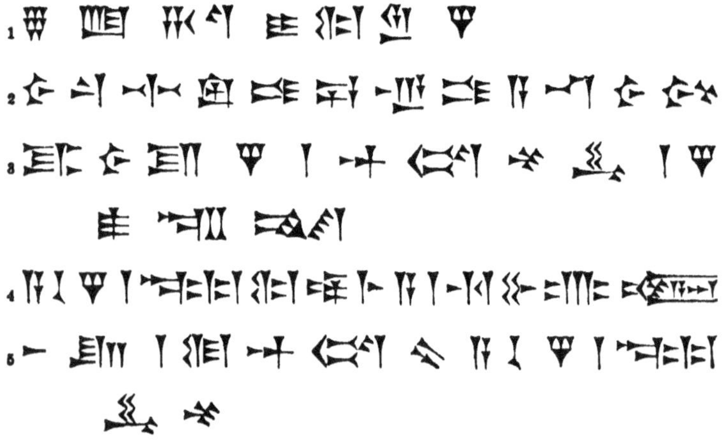

BACK.

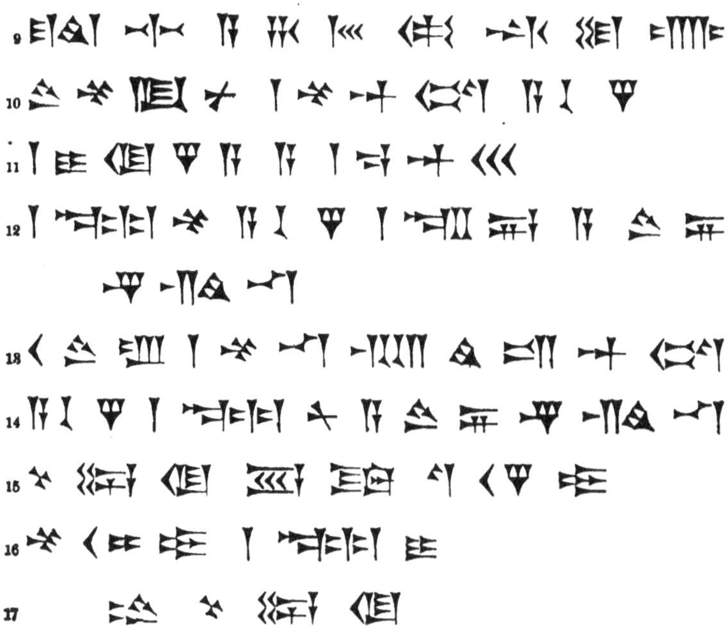

Tablet of a dark gray color. 1⅓ x 1⅙ inches. The writing is very much effaced; in fact, the tablet is gradually crumbling to pieces. The left side, as in most of these tablets, is not written upon. The above reading is the best possible.

Transliteration.

1 8 ṭu kaspi i-ṭi-ru ša

2 Ḳa-ti-lu-tum i-tir-tum a-na Amtu

3 marat-su ša Marduk-šum-uṣur Ša-aš-Bil-ṭi

Translation.

1 8 shekels of money, the pay which

2 Katilutum paid to Amtu,

3 the daughter of Mardukshumusur; Shâshbeltl,

4 apal-šu ša Nabû-itti-apli apal Ḫu-pu-u šimu	4 the son of Nabûittiapli, the son of Hupû, (his) price
5 ina ḳâtâ Itti-Marduk-balaṭu apal-šu ša Nabû-aḫi-iddin	5 from the hands of Ittimardukbalatu, the son of Nabûahiddin,
6 apal Î-gi-bi ma-ḫir	6 the son of Egibi, received.
7 i-pu-uš-ša duppa ša KI.LU libittu gi-nu-u u gišimmaru	7 They made a tablet concerning ......, bricks, offerings, and date palms,
8 a-di u.an.tim ša Nabû-aḫi-iddin	8 together with a receipt for Nabûahiddin.
9 it-ti a-ḫa-miš ul bal-tu-u	9 With one another not will they live.
10 amilu mu-kin-nu Iddin-Marduk apal-šu ša	10 Witness: Iddinmarduk, the son of
11 I-ki-ša-apla apal Nûr-Sin	11 Ikishâpla, the son of Nûrsin;
12 Nabû-iddin apal-šu ša Bil-idanin apal amilu ni-ṣur-gi-na	12 Nabûiddin, the son of Belidanin, the son of the ...... man;
13 u amilu dupsar Iddin-na-ḫu-nun-ṭi-iš-Marduk	13 and the scribe Iddinnahununtishmarduk,
14 apal-šu ša Nabû-naṣir apal amilu ni-ṣur-gi-na	14 the son of Nabûnasir, the son of the ...... man.
15 Babilu araḫ Nisannu ûmu 14 kam	15 Babylon, in the month Nisan, on the 14th day,
16 šattu 14 kam Nabû-na'id	16 in the 14th year of Nabûna'id,
17 šar Babili	17 King of Babylon.

NOTES.

1. i-ṭi-'u must be a substantive here, as the sense and every like construction demand. — 2. i-tir-tum, from the same root as the preceding, though a change in the first vowel has occurred. This form is also found in Strass. Nabn. 6'0' 17; 720, 15; Peiser, Bab. Ver. XLIII, 17; LXXI, 7. — Ša-aš-Bil-ṭi: we would expect Ša-aš-Bil-iṭ. The last sign, however, is indistinct on the tablet. — 4. Nabû-itti-apli: "May Nebo be with the sons." — 7. i-pu-uš-ša is in form the 3rd person plural feminine of the preterite. But there is no reason why the feminine should be used. I would again, as in 11, 6, regard it as a mistake that has crept into this the colloquial language of Babylon. It will be seen at the first glance how much the different cases are confounded, especially in the contract tablets. The Babylonian at this stage resembles the Middle Arabic, where the pronunciation of the final vowels was often kept, but where, in four cases out of five, the wrong ending was used, leading, in the end, to the dropping of all final vowels. KI.LU may perhaps be an ideogram for ṣinu "sheep." gi-nu-u is taken by Tallqvist (p. 62) to mean "sacrifices, offerings." Peiser (Bab. Ver. pp. 258 and 280) takes it as equivalent to alpi "cattle." See also Jeremias, B. A. I. p. 279. — 9. bal-tu-u: from balâṭu. As the ṭ and the t were almost identical in pronunciation, the scribe evidently did not make the distinction in this case. Tallqvist, on page 57 of his valuable little book, gives a word

balâtu "fulness, blessing," but this meaning evidently does not fit into this passage. — 12. amilu ni-ṣur-gi-na may mean "the man who guards the sacrificial offering;" from naṣâru "to protect" and ginû in line 7. He would thus be an attaché of the temple. — 13. The signs ḫu and nun are curiously blended together. — 16. Dated in the year 541 B. C.

The explanation of this text is easy. Katilutum and her husband Ittimardukbalatu determine to part with their servants Amtu and Shashbelti. The latter, I would conclude, are a married couple. Eight shekels are the wages of Amtu, and a similar amount, doubtlessly given on another tablet, came into the hands of Shashbelti. These four set up a tablet, giving the amount of work performed; and they add to this the receipt of Nabuahiddin, the father of Ittimardukbalatu, who therefore seems to have been the controlling power in the affairs of the two respective couples. This last receipt acted as a final document concerning their mutual relations; that is, it signified that the work had been properly performed, and that Ittimardukbalatu and his wife had to be satisfied and now had no claims against the servants. Finally, in line 9, we come to the quaint sentence: *With one another they will not live.* This shows that the rupture between the two couples is complete: they want to have nothing more to do with each other.

NO. 29.

FRONT.

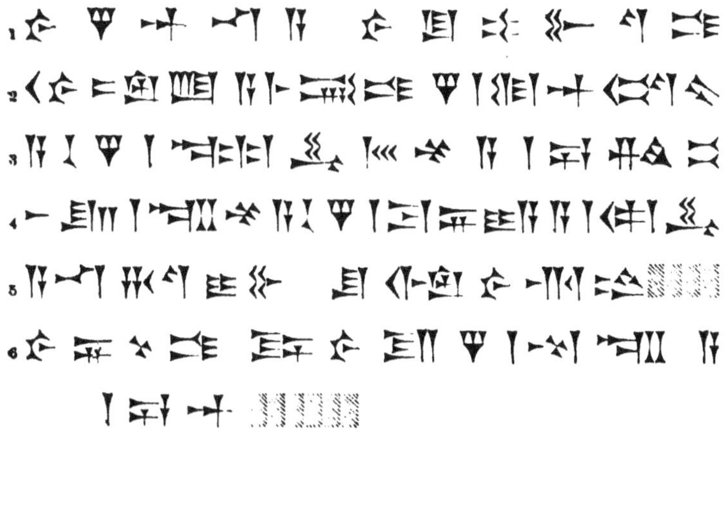

BACK.

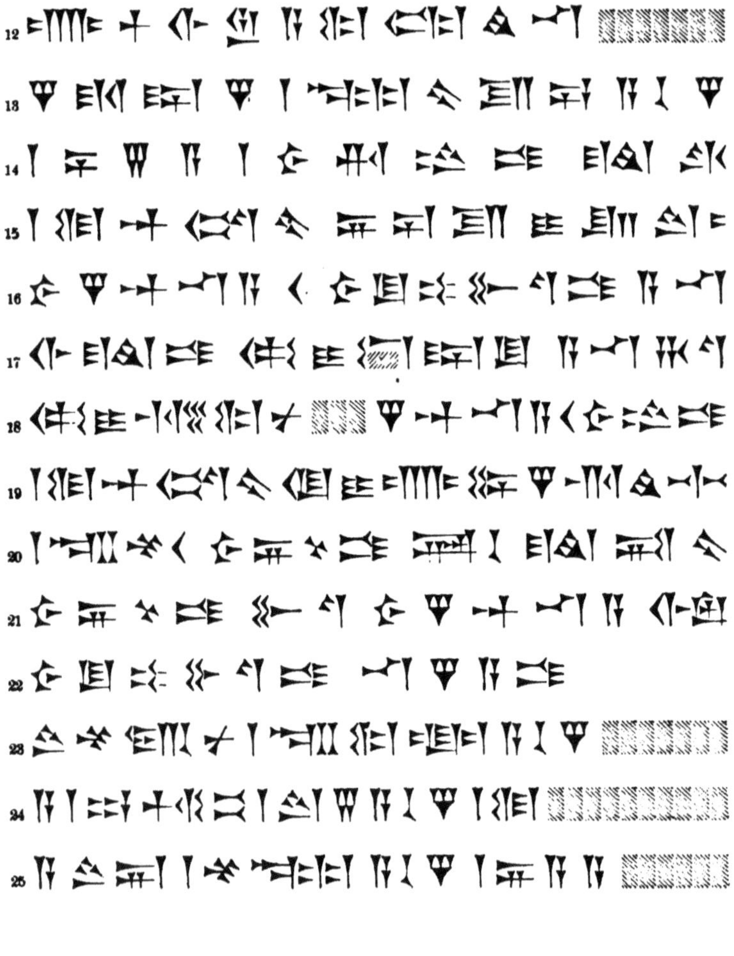

26 

LEFT SIDE.

27–30 

Tablet of a dark gray color, 1⅜ x 2¼ inches. The signs are very lightly made and closely written. In fact, the whole tablet is one conglomeration of signs, there being no space anywhere left unused. The scribe evidently sought to crowd as much as possible on the small piece of clay. On the right side, in some places, very little can be distinguished, as the signs are almost completely rubbed off. There is, however, but one break on the tablet, and this is in line 18, where the determinative for *woman* is broken out. The other lacunæ are caused by the rubbing off of the signs. The fact, that the scribe sought to crowd so long a text on so little space, accounts for the omission of many of the signs that must be supplied in order to make sense.

Transliteration.	*Translation.*
1 **Śa-an-na-a Ku-up-pu-ut-tum**	1 Shânnâ, Kûppûttum,
2 **u Tab-lu-ṭu a-mi-lut-tum śa Itti-Marduk-balaṭu**	2 and Tablutu, the slaves which Ittimar dukbalatu,
3 **apal-śu śa Nabû-aḫi-iddin apal Î-gi-bi**	3 the son of Nabûahiddin, the son of Egibi,
4 **ina ḳâtâ Bil-iddin apal-śu śa Ba-ni-ia apal Nirgal-uṣur**	4 from the hands of Beliddin, the son of Bania, the son of Nergalusur,
5 **a-na kaspi i-pu-śu u Ri-śar-[tum]**	5 for money received. And Rishartum (and)
6 **Ni-lat-tum marat-su śa Arad-Bil apal Iḳbi-[Marduk(?)]**	6 Nilattum, the daughter of Aradbel, the son of Ikbimarduk,
7 **u Bil-iddin apal-śu śa Ba-ni-ia apal Ri-śar-tum**	7 and Beliddin, the son of Bania, the son of Rishartum,
8 **kaspa śima pi-śa-an-na u Ku-up-pu-ut-tum**	8 for money, an equal price, and Kûppût-tum
9 **a-na Itti-Marduk-balaṭu id-di-nu u**	9 to Ittimardukbalatu gave; also
10 **Tab-lu-ṭu marat-su Ša-an-na-a**	10 Tablutu, the daughter of Shânnâ,

11 **a-di-i kaspi-šu id-din Itti-Marduk-balaṭu**	11 together with his money (that) he gave, Ittimardukbalatu
12 **u-maš-ši-ru adi ili na-[aš-ut-tu]**	12 left behind, until the bidding
13 **ša-ṭa-ra ša Nabû-balaṭ-su-iḳbi apal-šu ša**	13 in writing of Nabûbalatsuikbi, the son of
14 **Bani-ia apal Ri-šar-tum iṭ-bal**	14 Bania, the son of Rishartum, he will bring.
15 **Itti-Marduk-balaṭu ni-si-su i-kat-lul**	15 Ittimardukbalatu his bidding has fulfilled.
16 **Ša-an-na-a u Ku-up-pu-ut-tum a-na**	16 Shânnâ and Kûppûttum for
17 **ši-da-tum ul i-šar-ra-ku a-na kaspi**	17 a present not will he present (or) for money
18 **ul i-nam-di-nu Ša-an-na-a u [Ri]-šar-tum**	18 not will he sell. Shânnâ and Rishartum
19 **Itti-marduk-balaṭu ki-i u-tir ša ri-ḫi-ti**	19 Ittimardukbalatu, when he returns what remainder (there is),
20 **Bil-iddin u Ni-lat-tum ummi-šu it-ta-din**	20 (to) Beliddin and Nilattum, his mother, he will give.
21 **Ni-lat-tum pu-ut Ša-an-na-a u**	21 Nilattum the receipt (concerning) Shânnâ and
22 **Ku-up-pu-ut-tum na-ša-a-tum**	22 Kûppûttum will bring.
23 amilu **mu-kin-nu Bil-di-ḫir apal-šu ša**	23 Witnesses: Beldihir, the son of ......,
24 **apal Nab-iḳ-bi Ar-di-ia apal-šu ša Itti-**	24 the son of Nabikbi; Ardia, the son of Itti......,
25 **apal** amilu **šakânu Iddin-Nabû apal-šu ša Ṣal-a apal**	25 the son of the overseer: Iddinnabû, the son of Sala, the son of ......;
26 **Itti-Nabû-balaṭu** amilu **dupsar apal-šu ša Marduk-iddin**	26 Ittinabûbalatu, the scribe, the son of Mardukiddin,
27 **apal Bil-i-ṭi-ru**	27 the son of Beleteru.
28 **Babilu araḫ Nisannu ûmu 20 kam**	28 Babylon, in the month Nisan, on the 20th day,
29 **šattu 14 kam Nabû-na'id**	29 in the 14th year of Nabûna'id,
30 **šar Babili**	30 King of Babylon.

NOTES.

1. **a-mi-lut-tum** and **gallu** are used interchangeably. — 4. The determinative ilu "god" is omitted before **Nirgal**. — 5. The space in the word **i-pu—šu** denotes an erasure by the scribe on the tablet. "And" must be supplied at the end of the line, as **Rišartum** and **Nilattum** were two different women. — 8. **pi-ša-an-na-a** "equal;" compare the Hebrew פסס "to divide," hence "to divide into equal parts," then, "equal." **pi-ša-an-na** in Strass. Nabn. 186, 5; 213, 2; 1029, 7 is undoubtedly the same word. — 11. Notice

how peculiarly **id-din** is written. The horizontal wedge has the value of **nadânu**, and the three slanting wedges must here be taken as the phonetic complement **din**: giving us as the complete word the form **iddin**. — 13. **ša-ṭa-ra** I would take here as an adverbial accusative, or as an accusative of specification. Compare שְׁטַר and سطر. — 14. **iṭ-bal**. Ifteal of **abâlu**. — 15. **ni-ši-šu**. Perhaps this might be a secondary form of **našûtu** "bidding" from **našû**. That the **š** should go over into **s** would not be a strange thing in colloquial language. However, I offer this only as a suggestion. — 17. **ši-da-tum** I would connect with **šidû** "tribute," cf. Sanh. II, 55. It fits especially well with **i-šar-ra-ku**, from **šarâḳu** "to give, present," though the former is spelled with **k** and the latter with **ḳ**. — 18. **Ri-šar-tum**. **Ri** is omitted by the scribe by mistake: also the two combined vertical wedges at the end of the sign **tir** in line 19. — 20. **ana** must be supplied at the beginning of this line. — 24. **Nab-iḳ-bi**, a contracted form of **Nabû-iḳbi**. It is strange that the scribe has not recognized this and written the god's name with the determinative. I consider this a good example of how the Assyrian proper names were read. I believe that Nabû in proper names was read as it is here, and not, as in other cases, we are accustomed to transcribe it. But as Assyrian is a written and not a spoken language for us, we must transcribe the signs as they stand. — 28. The **sus.** sign **din** is omitted before **Babilu**. — 29. Dated in the year 541 B. C., as the preceding tablet.

The sense of the tablet is briefly the following. Ittimardukbalatu has been commissioned by Nabubalatsuikbi to acquire for him the three female slaves Shanna, Kupputtum, and Tablutu. Rishartum and Nilattum and Beliddin, who seem to have had some interest in the slave Kupputtum, hereby signify their assent to the sale. But Ittimardukbalatu is first required to show on what authority he purchases the slaves. He therefore leaves Tablutu and Shanna behind him as security, and deposits the money in order to bind the bargain, and goes to obtain a tablet from Nabubalatsuikbi, giving him authority to purchase the slaves. Probably Ittimardukbalatu was no responsible person, hence this demand was made. He is also required by the sellers neither to present the slaves to anybody, nor to sell them. The latter seem to have had a kind heart, for this condition was made, evidently, in order to protect the slaves from ever obtaining an unkind and cruel master. Ittimardukbalatu, when he returns the "change" to his employer, will finally hand over the purchase money to Beliddin and his mother, and will receive from the latter a receipt for two of the slaves. About the final disposal of the third slave, the want of room prevented the scribe from giving us any information. We are therefore compelled to wait for another tablet on this subject.

NO. 30.

FRONT.

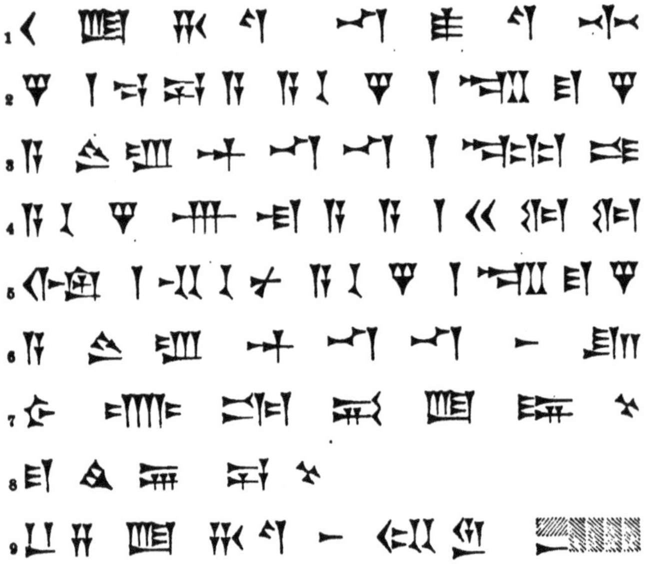

BACK.

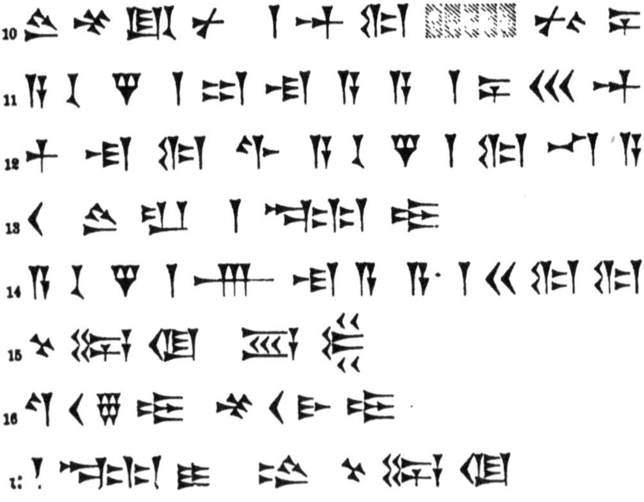

Tablet of a light maroon color. 1¼ x 1⅜ inches. The signs are blurred and difficult to decipher. The left side is not inscribed. In the first line of the reverse there is a large hole, which destroys the lower part (the vertical wedge) of the sign *tar*.

Transliteration.	*Translation.*
1 10 ṭu kaspi na-aš-ut-ti	1 10 shekels of money, the bidding
2 ša Nûr-i-a apal-šu ša Bil-iḳi-ša	2 of Nûrea, the son of Belikisha,
3 apal amilu šangu ilu Na-na Nabû-iriš	3 the son of the priest of Nana; Nabûeresh,
4 apal-šu ša Ṣil-la-a apal Man-di-di	4 the son of Sillâ, the son of Mandidi;
5 u Bil-šu-nu apal-šu ša Bil-iḳi-ša	5 and Belshunu, the son of Belikisha,
6 apal amilu šangu ilu Na-na ina ḳâtâ	6 the son of the priest of Nana, from the hands of
7 U-ka-ga-tu-ra-šad	7 Ukagaturashad
8 ma-ḫi-ir i-lat	8 have received; in addition
9 1/3 4 ṭu kaspi ina gim-ru	9 4⅓ shekels of money in vegetables (she paid?).
10 amilu mu-kin-nu ilu Dainu-zir-ibni	10 Witnesses: Dainuziribni,
11 apal-šu ša Ab-la-a apal Ipi-iš-ilu	11 the son of Ablâ, the son of Epêshilu;
12 La-di-pi apal-šu ša Di-na-a	12 Ladipi, the son of Dinâ,
13 u amilu dupsar Nabû-iriš	13 and the scribe Nabûeresh,
14 apal-šu ša Ṣil-la-a apal Man-di-di	14 the son of Sillâ, the son of Mandidi.
15 Babilu araḫ Simanu	15 Babylon, in the month Simanu,
16 ûmu 18 kam šattu 14 kam	16 on the 18th day, in the 14th year of
17 Nabû-na'id šar Babili	17 Nabûna'id, King of Babylon.

NOTES.

8. **ma-ḫi-ir** is the singular; we would expect the plural. **i-lat**: see note to 13, 11. — 9. **gim-ru**: see Tallqvist p. 61. The latter takes it to be the name of some produce mentioned together with grain and vegetables. — 10. **ilu Dainu-zir-ibni.** The fourth sign of the name is tar; in Brünnow's Classified List (No. 9541) the reading is not given. The above is only tentative. — 12. The first sign is evidently a mistake on the part of the scribe. The sense requires that only the vertical wedge should stand here. The wedge crossing it is out of place. The family name of the last witness is omitted. — 16. Dated in the year 541 B. C., as the two preceding tablets.

Ukagaturashad had embarked in the grocery business. She had received a commission from Nurea, Nabutum, and Belshunu to furnish 10 shekels worth of groceries as well as 4⅓ shekels worth of vegetables. She acquitted herself of this commission, and obtained this tablet as a receipt.

NO. 31.

FRONT.

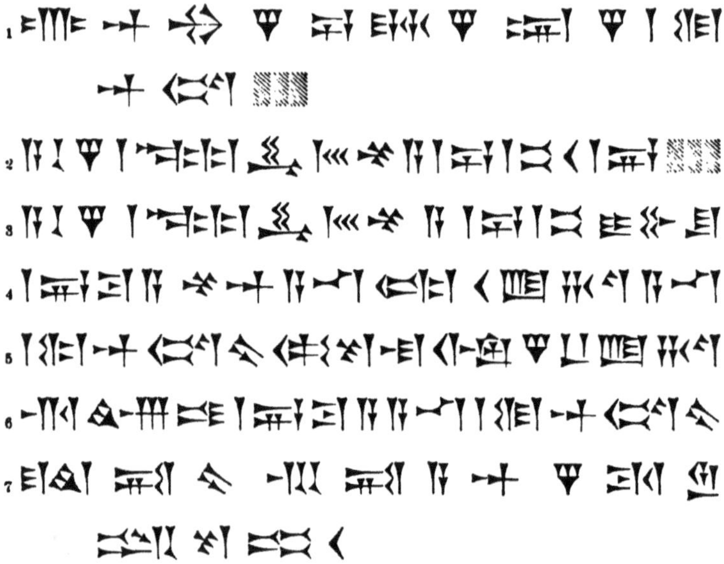

BACK.

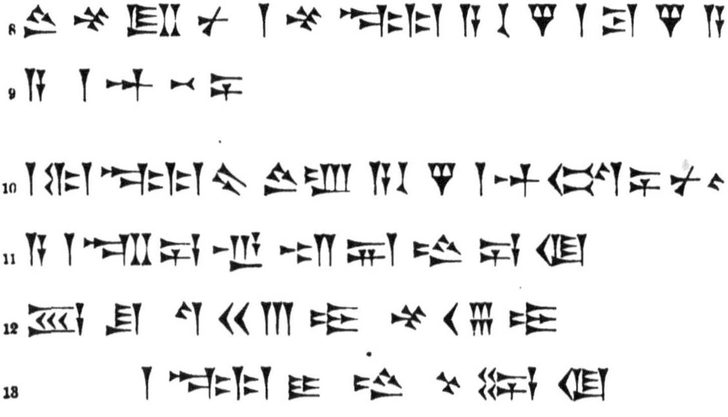

Tablet of a light fawn color, 1¾ x 2 inches. The signs are very small and, in some places, indistinctly made. The writing is divided into three parts: First, the obverse, giving the subject matter of the tablet, with a large space below, which extends to the top of the reverse. Secondly, one and one-third lines on the upper part of the reverse, which contain the name and parentage of but one witness. Below this there is again a large space. Finally, four lines containing the name of the scribe and the date. This careful division of the text shows that the scribe must have been a painstaking man.

None of the sides is written upon. The right hand upper corner of the obverse is broken off, otherwise the tablet would be complete.

Transliteration.	*Translation.*
1 **u.an.tim ša i-piš-ša duppu ša Itti-Marduk-[balaṭu]**	1 The receipt which is made out (namely) the tablet, which Ittimardukbalatu,
2 **apal-šu ša Nabû-aḫi-iddin apal Î-gi-bi u [Kal-ba-a]**	2 the son of Nabûahiddin, the són of Egibi, and Kalbâ,
3 **apal-šu ša Nabû-aḫi-iddin apal Î-gi-bi i-pu-šu**	3 the son of Nabûahiddin, the son of Egibi, made.
4 **Kal-ba-a šatta ili 10 ṭu kaspi a-na**	4 Kalbâ every year about 10 shekels of money to
5 **Itti-Marduk-balaṭu ul-ti-la u 4 1/2 ṭu kaspi**	5 Ittimardukbalatu will pay, and 4½ shekels of money,
6 **ri-'ḫ-tum Kal-ba-a a-na Itti-Marduk-balaṭu**	6 the remainder, Kalbâ unto Ittimardukbalatu
7 **it-ta-din išti-in ta.a.an ša-ṭa-ru il-ti-ḳu-u**	7 will give. One document they took.
8 **^{amilu} mu-kin-nu Iddin-Nabû apal-šu ša Iḳi-ša-apla**	8 Witness: Iddinnabû, the son of Ikishapla,
9 **apal Bil-ibni**	9 the son of Belibni.
10 **Itti-Nabû-balaṭu ^{amilu} dupsar apal-šu ša Marduk-ban-zir**	10 Ittinabûbalatu, the scribe, the son of Mardukbanzir,
11 **apal Bil-iṭir alu Bit-šar-i ^{irṣitu}**	11 the son of Beleter. In the city Bitshare,
12 **araḫ Dûzu ûmu 23 kam šattu 16 kam**	12 in the month Dûzu, on the 23 rd day, in the 16 th year of
13 **Nabû-na'id šar ^{mat} Babili**	13 Nabûna'id, King of Babylon.

NOTES.

4. **šatta.** Note the insertion of an a between the signs **an** and **na**. All four signs must be read as an ideogram. — 5. **ul-ti-la** for **uš-ila**: Ifteal of **ilu**. — 7. **il-ti-ḳu-u**: Ifteal of **liḳu**. — 8. As a general rule two or more witnesses were required for every legal action; here only one is mentioned. The scribe, however, can be considered the second. — 12. Dated in the year 539 B. C.

Two brothers, Kalba and Ittimardukbalatu, enter into an agreement concerning the disposal of certain funds, perhaps left to them by their deceased father. Kalba seems to possess a generous heart, for he promises his brother a yearly support of 10 shekels, besides giving him the remainder left over from the money inherited from his father.

PART II.

NO. 1.

OBVERSE.

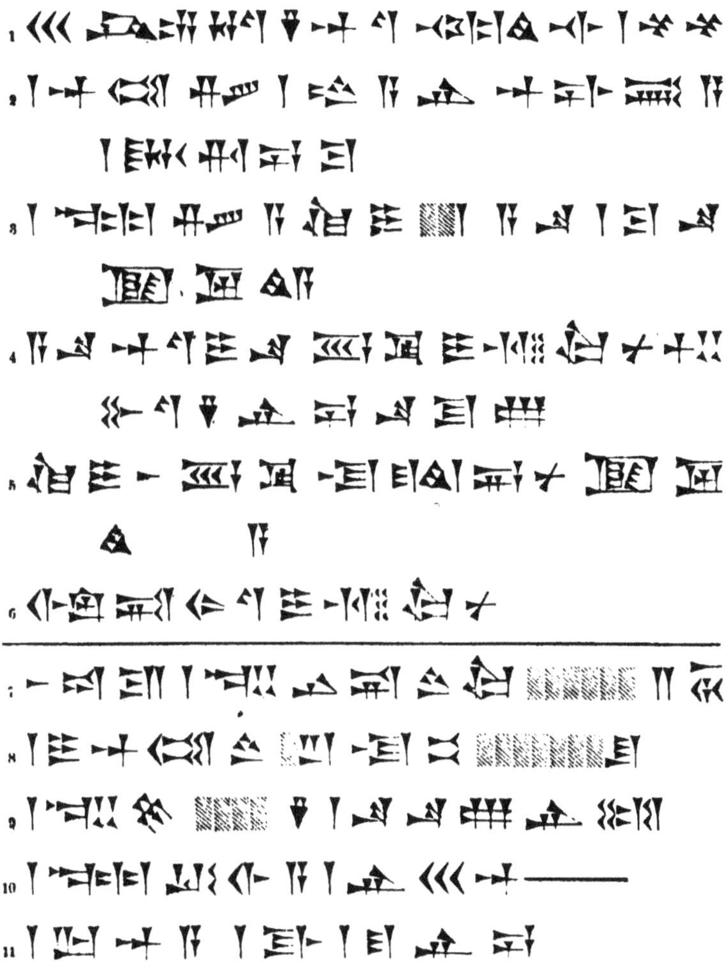

REVERSE.

14 

Tablet light brown, beautifully glazed. The obverse is very much effaced by cracks and breaks, but the reverse is perfect 1¾×2¼ inches. The signs are beautifully made. Line 4 is prolonged over the right edge. The king's name in the last line is very plain.

1 30 *biltum kaspi ša Šamaš ina ili ina pân Šum-iddin*	1 Thirty talents of money, belonging to Shamash, to be received of Shumiddin,
2 *Marduk-musallim Šar-a-ni-Mar-duk-apal Kir-ri-i-ma*	2 Mardukmusallim, Sharrâuimarduk-apal, Kirrêma, (and)
3 *Nabû-musallim a-ki-i-ma a-na* 1 *ma-na ṣinî*	3 Nabûmusallim. Accordingly, for one mana sheep
4 *a-na Šamaš i-na araḫ Ululu i-nam-di-nu išti-în pu-ut ša-ni-i na-šu-u*	4 to Shamash in the month Ululu they will give. One for the other is security.
5 *ki-i ina araḫ Ululu lâ id-dan-nu ṣinî*	5 If in the month Ululu they will not give (them), the sheep
6 *u la-lit-tu i-nam-di-nu*	6 and the young (?) they will give.
7 *ina manzazu Bil-ipu-uš (amilu) dainu*	7 In the presence of Belepûsh, the judge ... ...;
8 *Na'id-Marduk (amilu) šangu la bi*	8 Na'idmarduk, the priest ....;
9 *Bil-iriš [apal-šu] ša Na-na-u-ni-li*	9 Belerêsh, the son of Nanaunili;
10 *Nabû-gal-lim apal Ipi-iš-ilu*	10 Nabûgallim, the son of Epêshilu;
11 *Arad-ilu apal Rab-diš-bani-i*	11 Aradilu, the son of Rabdishbanê;
12 *u (amilu) dupsar Nabû-itir-napšâti Nippuru*	12 and the scribe Nabûetêrnapshâti. Nippur,
13 *ûmu 13 kam šattu riš šarrûtu*	13 on the 13th day, in the accession year of
14 *Sin-šum-lîšir šar (mat) Aššur(ki)*	14 Sinshumlishir, King of Assyria.

Thirty talents of money are due the god Shamash, or rather his temple at Nippur (Niffer). On the strength of this the six persons mentioned in lines 1, 2, and 3, are to pay tithes. They are to present the god in the month Ululu (September) with sheep, to the value of one mana. If they fail to bring the tithe in the stipulated time, they are to give the sheep and their increase, probably at a time when the priests become tired of waiting.

This is the only tablet of the collection dated in the reign of a king of Assyria. As a king of this name is as yet unknown to me, I should prefer to call him one of Asurbanipal's successors, about whom there is still much to be learned.

NO. 2.

OBVERSE.

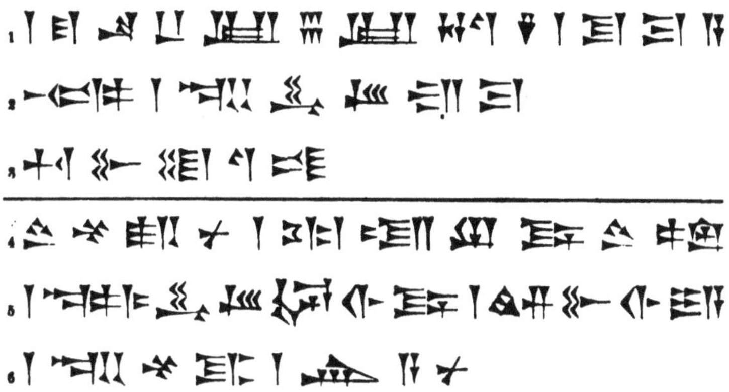

REVERSE.

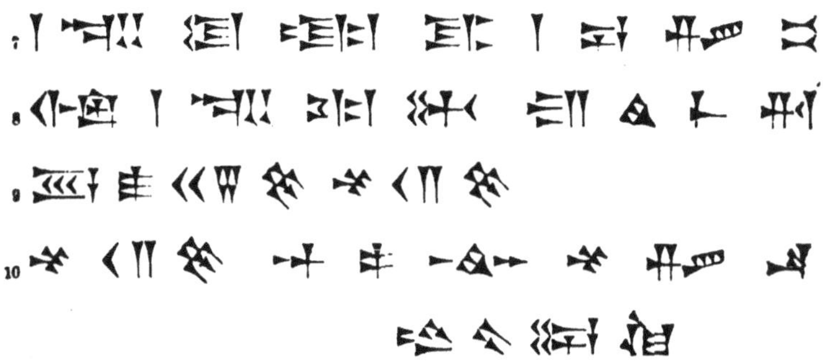

Tablet yellow, 1⅝×2⅛ inches. In perfect state of preservation, The signs are large and well made. The upper edge and also the left edge are without writing; the right edge contains a few signs of prolonged lines. Below line 3 there is a line separating the first three lines, as indicated above, from the rest of the tablet.

1 1 *ma-na* ⅓ *šiḳlu* 6 *šiḳlu kaspi ša Šu-la-a*	1 One mana, one-third shekel and six shekels of money, which Shulâ
2 *ina ili Bil-aḫî-ir-ba*	2 is to receive from Belahirba
3 *ḫu-bu-ṭu-ut-tum*	3 as advance.

4 *(amîlu) mu-kin-nu Ka-ṣi-ru mâr (amîlu) ri'u*	4 Witnesses: Kasiru, the son of the shepherd;
5 *Nabû-aḫî-šul-lim mâr Im-bu-ši-ia*	5 Nabûahishullim, the son of Imbushia;
6 *Bil-iddin mâr Ir-a-nu*	6 Beliddin, the son of Iranu;
7 *Bil-ki-šir mâr Í-gi-bi*	7 Belkishir, the son of Egibi;
8 *u Bil-ka-ṣir alû Ḫi-mi-ri*	8 and Belkasir. At the city Himeri,
9 *araḫ Šabaṭu* [*ûmu*] 25 *kam šattu* 12 *kam*	9 in the month Shabatu, on the 25th day, in the 12th year,
10 *šattu* 12 *kam Šamaš-šum-ukin-na*	10 in the 12th year of Shamashshum-ukin,
11 *šar Babili(ki)*	11 King of Babylon.

Shulâ has advanced Belahirba 1 mana and 6⅓ shekels, and this tablet merely records that fact without stating when the money is to be returned, or what interest, if any, is to be paid.

NO. 3.

OBVERSE.

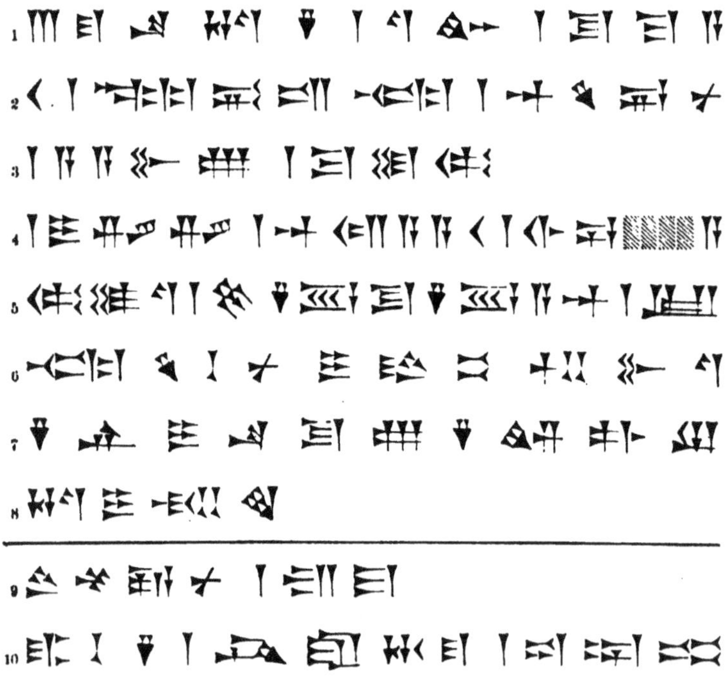

REVERSE.

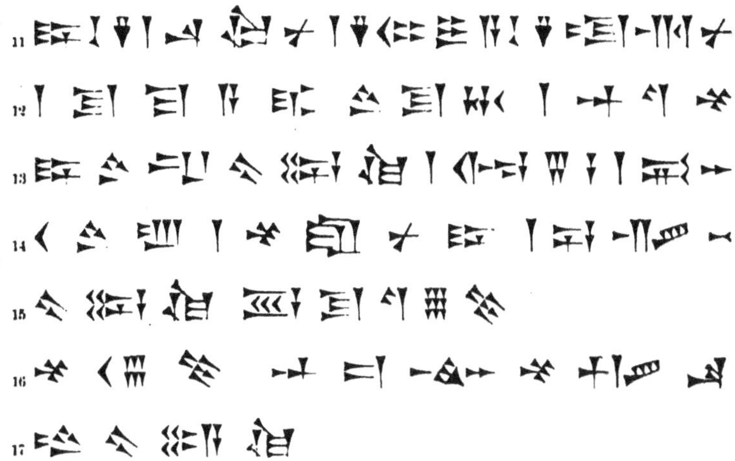

Tablet brown, mottled with black spots; 1¾×2¼ inches. The obverse is flat, while the reverse curves outward, so that the tablet is one inch thick at the middle. Perfectly preserved. The signs are large and well made There is a large space at the end not used, and the left edge is also without writing.

1 *3 ma-na kaspi ša Tu-' Šu-la-a*	1 Three mana of money which Tu', Shulâ,
2 *u Nabû-ga-mil ina ili Aššur-dan-nu*	2 and Nabûgamil are to receive from Ashshurdannu,
3 *Ai-bu-u Ba-tu-ul*	3 Aibû, Batûl,
4 *I-gi-gi Nergal-ai u Ši-i-[gu-a]*	4 Igigi, Nergalai, and Shêgua.
5 *ultu ûmu 1 kam ša araḫ Dûzu ša arḫa.a.an 1 šiḳlu*	5 From the first day of the month Dûzu on, every month one shekel
6 *ina ili-šu-nu i-rab-bi išti-in pu-ut*	6 against them shall increase. One is security for
7 *ša-ni-i na-šu-u ša im-mar-ru*	7 the other. Whom they will find,
8 *kaspu i-maḫ-ḫar*	8 he shall receive the money.
9 *(amilu) mu-kin-nu Ir-ba*	9 Witnesses: Irba,
10 *mâr-šu ša Tik-ra-ḫa-ma Du-um-ḳu*	10 the son of Tikrahama; Dumku,
11 *mâr-šu ša Ḳa-di-nu Ša-mi-i apal-šu ša Ad-ri-nu*	11 the son of Kadinu; Shamî, the son of Adrinu;
12 *Šu-la-a mâr (amilu) bâ'iru Šamaš-iddin*	12 Shulâ, the son of the fisherman; Shamashiddin,
13 *mâr (amilu) šangu Babili(ki) Dumḳi-ia apal Ga-ḫal*	13 the son of the priest of Babylon; Dumkia, the son of Gahal;

14 *u (amilu) dupsar Mu-ra-nu mâr Î-gi-bi*	14 **and the scribe, Muranu, the son of Egibi.**
15 *Babilu(ki) araḫ Dûzu ûmu 9 kam*	15 **Babylon, in the month Dûzu, on the 9th day,**
16 *šattu 16 kam Šamaš-šum-ukin-na*	16 **in the 16th year of Shamashshum-ukin,**
17 *šar Babili(ki)*	17 **King of Babylon.**

The three persons named in lines 1 and 2, have loaned three mana to the six mentioned in lines 3 and 4. They are to pay no interest till the month Dûzu (July) arrives. Thereafter they must pay the very moderate interest of one shekel per month, that is, 6⅔ per cent per year. If, however, the debtors wish to return the money, they may pay it to any one of the three creditors, whom they can most conveniently reach.

NO. 4.

OBVERSE.

REVERSE.

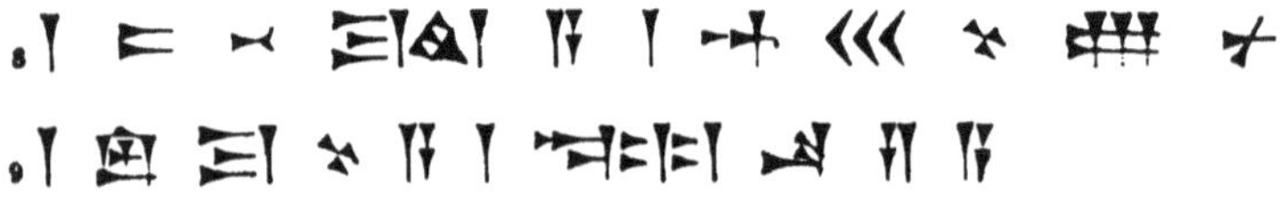

Tablet yellow; 1⅛×2 inches. The signs are very indistinct, as if the stylus used was dull or had been pressed into the clay lightly. The two names at the beginning of lines 8 and 9 are but tentative readings, as they are partially covered with a hard flinty substance. The edges are not written upon. A large space is left between lines 9 and 10.

1 ⅓ *šiḳlu kaspi ni-is-ḫu*	1 One-third shekel of money, the revocation,
2 *ša ili Nabû-bil-ilâni*	2 which (took place) against Nabûbelilâni,
3 *ul-tu ûmu* 20 *kam ša araḫ Dûzu*	3 from the 20th day of the month Dûzu,
4 *a-šar Nabû-šum-iškun-un ina pân a-mur-a*	4 wherever Nabûshumishkun will be found,
5 *u-tir li-iṭ-ṭir*	5 the remainder he will verily return.
6 (*amilu*) *mu-kin-nu Sil-la-a*	6 Witnesses: Sillâ,
7 *mâr ša Nabû-na-ai*	7 the son of Nabûnâai;
8 *Tab-bi-it apal Sin-kur-u-nu*	8 Tabêt, the son of Sinkurunu;
9 *Lu-ba-laṭ apal Nabû-na-ai*	9 Lubalat, the son of Nabûnâai;
10 *u* (*amilu*) *dupšar Šamaš-u-ši-zib*	10 and the scribe Shamashushezib.
11 *Babilu*(*ki*) *araḫ Dûzu ûmu* 20 *kam*	11 Babylon, in the month Dûzu, on the 20th day,
12 *šattu* 16 *kam Šamaš-šum-ukin*	12 in the 16th year of Shamashshumukin,
13 *šar Babili*(*ki*)	13 King of Babylon.

Nabûbelilâni had been excluded by Nabûshumishkun from a certain portion of his inheritance. Now this action is revoked and Nabûbelilâni can hope to inherit all he had expected.

NO. 5.

OBVERSE.

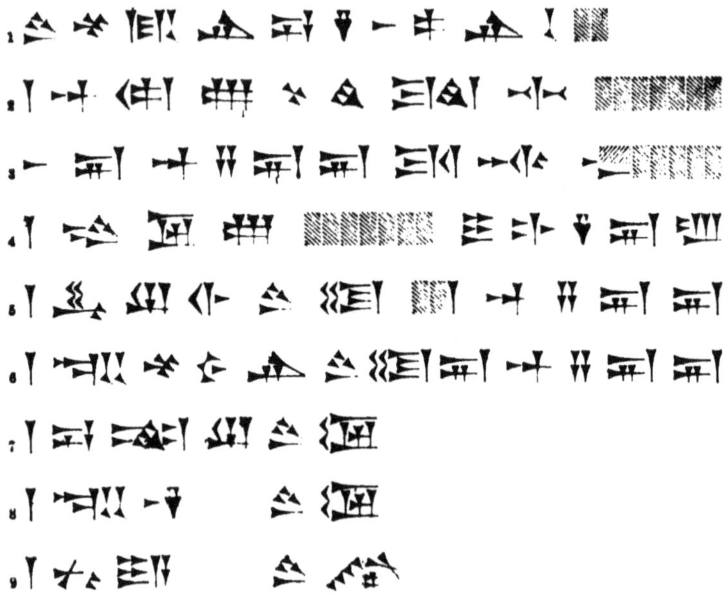

REVERSE.

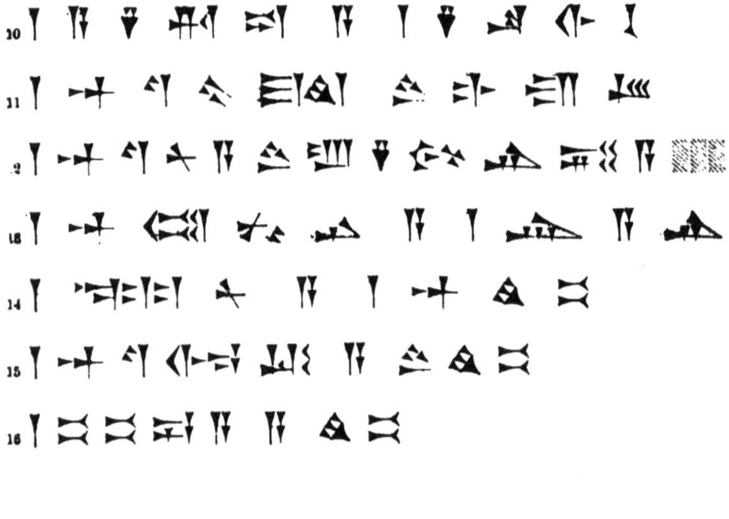

Tablet brown shading to black; $1\frac{1}{2}\times2\frac{1}{4}$ inches. The upper right hand corner of the obverse is destroyed, and the obverse is badly damaged throughout by the crumbling off of the clay. The reverse is almost perfect, a few easily supplied signs at the end of lines 17 and 18 being broken off. The signs are very plain. There is no writing on the left edge.

1 *(amilu) mu-kin-ni-i ša ina pa-ni-šu-[nu]*	1 These are the witnesses according to whose testimony
2 *Nergal-u-šat-hi it-ti*	2 Nergalushathi with........
3 *ina bît (ilu) Ṣa-bit-bit ta-bal-[la-aṭ]*	3 in the temple of the god Sabitbit lived.
4 *Šar-lu-u-* .... *i-pi-ša Í.DUP*	4 Sharlû..........................
5 *Uṣur-ru-ši (amilu) TU [biti] (ilu) Ṣa-bit-bit*	5 Usurrushi, the........of the temple of the god Sabitbit;
6 *Bil-mu-šal-ni (amilu) TU biti (ilu) Ṣa-bit-bit*	6 Belmushalni, the .... of the temple of the god Sabitbit;
7 *Í-ṭi-ru (amilu) TU biti (ilu) Ṣa-bit-bit*	7 Etêru, the........of the temple of the god Sabitbit;
8 *Bil-iṭir? (amilu) TU biti (ilu) Ṣa-bit-bit*	8 Beletêr, the........of the temple of the god Sabitbit;
9 *Zir-ia (amilu) zammaru*	9 Ziria, the singer;
10 *A-ša-ri-du apal Ša-na-ši-šu*	10 Asharidu, the son of Shanashishu;
11 *Šamaš-uballi-iṭ (amilu) PI.IR.MIŠ*	11 Shamashuballit, the..... ..;
12 *Šamaš-uṣur (amilu) šangu ša Amat-ni-gab-a[(ki)]*	12 Shamashusur, the priest of the city (?) Amatnigaba;
13 *Marduk-zir-ibni apal Ir-a-ni*	13 Mardukziribni, the son of Irani;
14 *Nabû-uṣur apal Aššur-itmi*	14 Nabûsur, the son of Ashshuritmi;
15 *Šamaš-mudammi-iḳ apal (amilu) ḪI.BI*	15 Shamashmudammik, the son of the.... ...;
16 *Bi-bi-i-a apal (amilu) ḪI.BI*	16 Bibêa, the son of the...............
17 *araḫ Tašritu ûmu 17 kam šattu 13 k[am]*	17 In the month Tashritu, on the 17th day, in the 13th year of
18 *Kan-ṭa-la-nu šar Ba[bili(ki)]*	18 Kineladanos, King of Babylon.

This tablet is evidently a document prepared for use in some suit. It gives the names of the witnesses who could testify that Nergalushathi and another person, whose name is contained in the break at the end of line 2, had lived together in the temple of the god Sabitbit for a certain time. What the two words at the end of line 4 mean, I am at loss to say, as the meaning of *Í. DUP* is not known.

The name of the king, Kineladanos, has been frequently identified with Assurbanipal, and many Assyriologists argue that the latter, after the overthrow of his brother Shamashshumukin, ruled over Babylon in person, assuming this obscure name Kineladanos. But this seems impossible. We cannot understand how an illustrious Assyrian king should lay aside that illustrious name and assume an insignificant and unknown one. Kineladanos is most likely the predecessor of Nabopolassar on the throne of Babylon.

NO. 6.

OBVERSE.

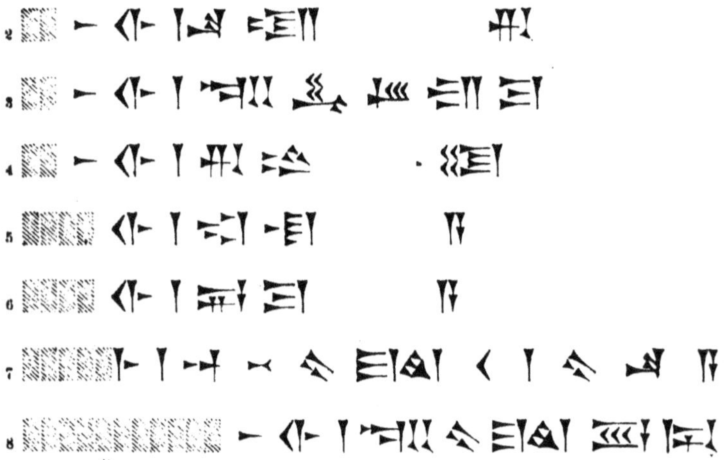

About two lines on the obverse, and two on the reverse are broken off.

REVERSE.

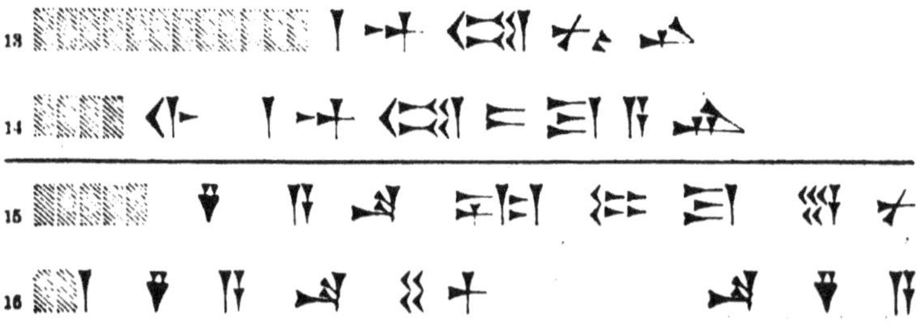

Tablet light brown; 1⅝×2¼ inches. A fragment. The lower and left portions are completely destroyed, as well as line 1. The signs have also suffered considerably. Line 4 seems to have been erased.

2 ...... *ina pân Na-ṣi-ri*	2 ...... from Nasiri;
3 ...... *ina pân Bil-aḫi-ir-ba*	3 ...... from Belahirba;
4 ...... *ina pân Ri-šar-tu*	4 ...... from Rishartu;
5 ...... *[ina] pân Šu-la-a*	5 ...... from Shulâ;
6 ...... *[ina] pân Kal-ba-a*	6 ...... from Kalbâ;
7 ...... *[ina p]ân Bil-uballi-iṭ u Dir-na-a*	7 ...... from Beluballit and Dinnâ;
8 .... *ina pân Bil-uballi-iṭ araḫ Ululu*	8 ...... from Baluballit; in the month Ululu (they will pay).

Lines 9–12 are destroyed.

13 ...... *[ina pân] Marduk-zir-ibni*	13 ...... from Marduk:iribni;
14 ...... *[ina] pân Marduk-tab-ba-a-ni*	14 ...... from Marduktabbâni.
15 ...... *ša a-na sulûpu iddin-nu*	15 ...... which for dates were given;
16 ...... *ša a-na ŠI.BAR na-ša-a*	16 ...... which for grain were brought;
17 ...... *ma-na 50 šiḳlu 3½ šiḳlu kaspi*	17 ...... mana 53½ shekels of money;
18 ...... *[u] 16 ma-na 14 šiḳlu ta.[a.an]. mlš kaspi*	18 and 16 mana 14 shekels each of money.
19 ...... *[araḫ Air]u ûmu 15 kam šattu 14 kam*	19 In the month Airu, on the 15th day, in the 14th year of
20 ...... *Kan-ṭa-la-nu*	20 Kineladanos.

The clew to this tablet, the first line, is unfortunately broken off. But it is plain that it contains a list of some objects, which the persons mentioned in lines 2–14 are to pay either as tithes or as taxes. The parts broken off at the beginning of lines 2—17 evidently contained numerals. Line 17 seems to imply that the dates mentioned in line 15 were valued at .. mana 53½ shekels; and the grain, in line 16, according to line 18, at 16 mana, 14 shekels.

NO. 7.

OBVERSE.

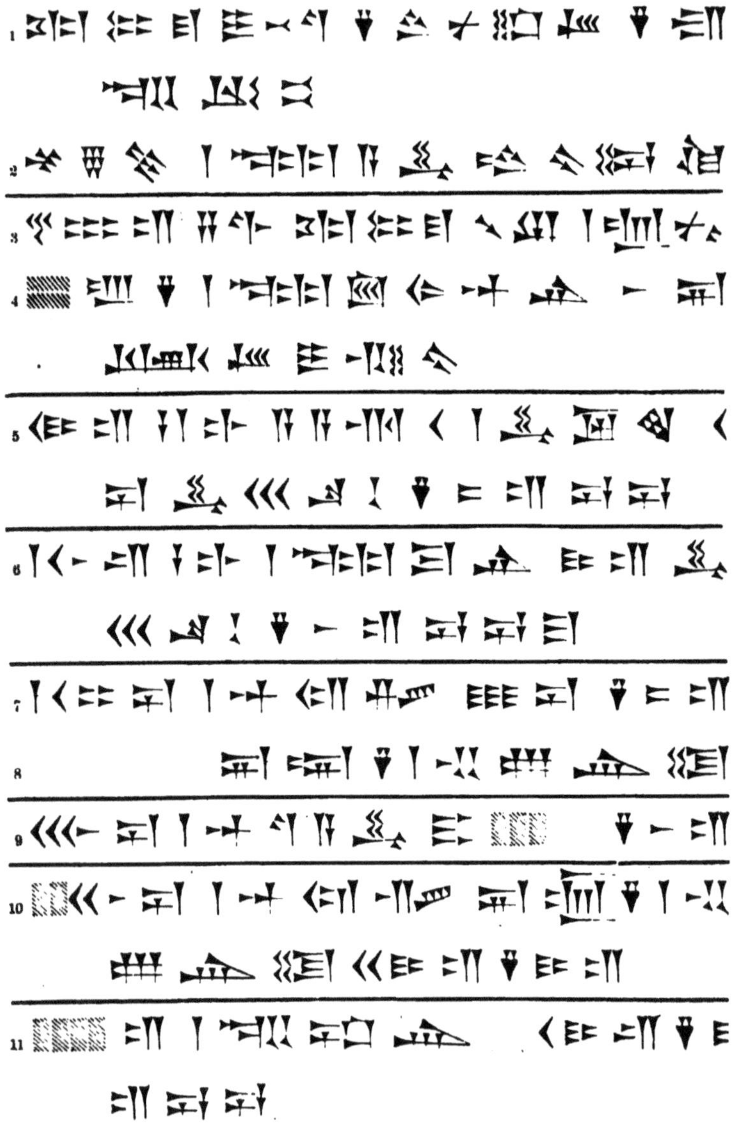

REVERSE.

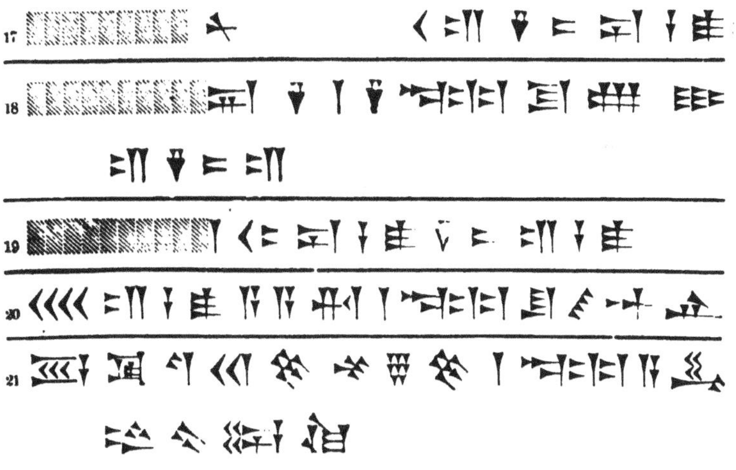

Tablet brown; 2⅞×3¼ inches. The lower left hand corner of the obverse is totally broken off, also the upper left hand corner of the reverse is destroyed thus. The tablet is in bad condition, cracks, crumbling off of the clay, and breaks occur throughout. The upper and the left edges are not written upon. Erasures are frequent. A few wedges, numerals, are scattered in the empty space above and below the date on the reverse, not bearing upon the text of the tablet. Line 8 is written small and very closely to line 7, as if explanatory of line 7.

1 *sulûpu i-mil-tu ša (amîlu) NU:ŠAR. MÍŠ ša alû Bil-iḳ-bi*

2 *šattu 8 kam Nabû-apal-uṣur šar Babili (ki)*

3 46 *gur* 4 *pi sulûpu gam-ru Šapik-zir*

4 [*Í*].*DUP ša Nabû-bul-lit-an-ni ina bîti iburi i-nam-din*

5 15 *gur* 3 *pi Ai-ri u Aḫu-lu-mur* 10 *gur šiš-šin-na šu ša* 2 *gur i-ṭir* (*!*)

6 71 *gur* 2 *pi Nabû-ba-ni* 5 *gur šiš-šin-na-šu ša* 1 *gur i-ṭir-ma*

7 74 *gur Nirgal-musallim* 9 *gur ša* 2 *gur*

8 *Í.DUP ša Bil-u-ir-tu*

9 31 *gur Šamaš-apal-uṣur* 5 [*gur*] *ša* 1 *gur*

10 + 21 *gur Nirgal-musallim Í.DUP ša Bil-u-ir-tu* 25 *gur ša* 5 *gur*

11 .... *gur Bil-šaḳ-ir* 15 *gur ša* 3 *gur i-ṭir*

12 .... *Marduk-šum-ibni Šamaš ṣap-ir* 16 *gur* 2 *pi ša* 3 *gur* 2 *pi*

13 .... *u Nirgal-ibni Í.DUP ša Nabû-na'id*

14 .. ..*-ukin Í.DUP* 2 *gur ša* 3 *gur*

15 .... *Nabû-zir-ibni*

16 ....*-Bil Í.DUP ša Nabû-ibni-*[*zir*]

17 ....*-uṣur* 10 *gur ša* 2 *gur* 2 *pi*

1 Dates still on the tree, belonging to the .... officers of the city of Belikbi.

2 In the 8th year of Nabopolassar, King of Babylon.

3 46 gur 4 pi perfect dates Shapikzir,

4 as the .... of Nabûbullitanni, into the store-houses will give.

5 15 gur 3 pi (dates) Airi and Ahulumur, 10 gur of their palm branches equivalent to 2 gur (dates) they will give.

6 71 gur 2 pi (dates) Nabûbâni, 5 gur of his palm branches equivalent to 1 gur (dates) he will give.

7 74 gur (dates) Nergalmusallim, 9 gur (palm branches) equivalent to 2 gur (dates),

8 the .... of Beluirtu, (he will give).

9 31 gur (dates) Shamashapalusur, 5 gur (palm branches) equivalent to 1 gur (dates, he will give).

10 + 21 gur (dates) Nergalmusallim, the .... of Beluirtu, 25 gur (palm branches) equivalent to 5 gur (dates, he will give).

11 .... gur (dates) Belshakir, 15 gur (palm branches) equivalent to 3 gur (dates), he will give.

12 Mardukshumibni (and) Shamashsapir, 16 gur 2 pi (palm branches) equivalent to 3 gur 2 pi (dates, they will give).

13 .... and Nergalibni, the .... of Nabûna'id.

14 .... ukin, the .... 2 gur (palm branches) equivalent to 3 gur (dates).

15 .... Nabûziribni.

16 ....bel, the ...... of Nabû-ibnizir.

17 .... usur, 10 gur (palm branches) equivalent to 2 gur 2 pi (dates).

18 .... *[Í.D] UP ša Šu-Nabû-šu-u 8 gur ša 2 gur*

19 .... *12 gur 2 pi ša 2 gur 2 pi*

20 *40 gur 2 pi Ai-ri Nabû-šu-zib-an-ni*

21 *araḫ Ulula ûmu 21 kam šattu 8 kam Nabû-apal-uṣur šar Babili(ki)*

18 .... the ...... of Shanabúshû, 8 gur (palm branches) equivalent to 2 gur (dates).

19 .... 12 gur 2 pi (palm branches) equivalent to 2 gur 2 pi (dates).

20 40 gur 2 pi Airi (and) Nabûshuzibanni (will give).

21 In the month Ululu, on the 21st day, in the 8th year of Nabopolassar, King of Babylon.

This tablet treats of the taxes that the farmers had to pay to the granary of the city Belikbi. The officials mentioned in line 1, were probably the tax-gatherers. The tablet seems to say that palm branches could be used instead of the fruit in payment of the taxes, and the ratio between the value of the branches and of the fruit is given in several instances. The bad state of preservation in which the tablet now is, and the terse expressions, render the tablet difficult to translate.

NO. 8.

OBVERSE.

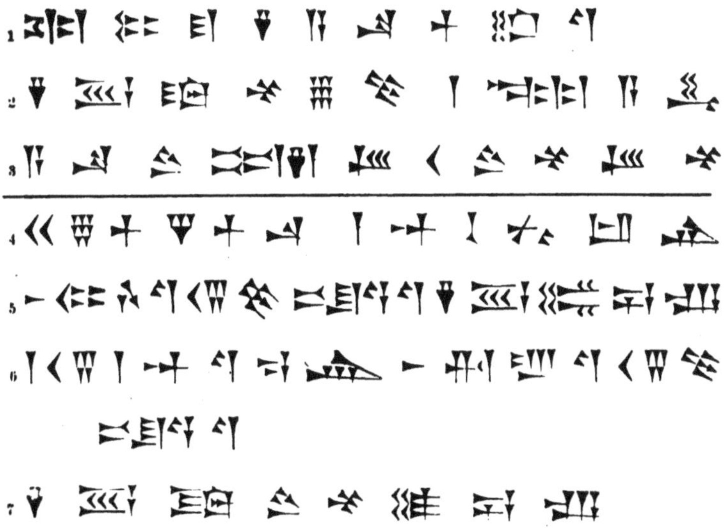

 *The remainder of the line is erased, the traces correspond to line* 11.

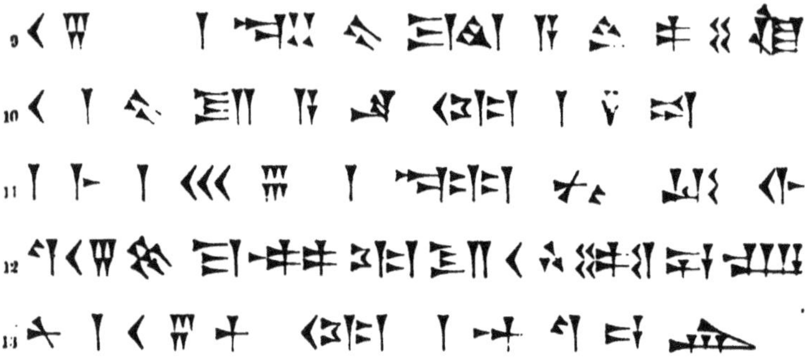

REVERSE.

Tablet gray; 1⅝×2⅛ inches. The clay is soft and brittle. The signs are very small and crude. A straight line separates lines 2 and 4. Line 13 just occupies the lower edge. There is much space wasted.

1 *sulûpu ša a-na maš-šar-tu*	1 (This is the number of measures of) dates, which at the end
2 *ša araḫ Nisannu šattu* 9 *kam Nabû-apal-uṣur*	2 of the month Nisanuu of the 9th year of Nabopolassar,
3 *a-na amîlu ......MÍŠ u (amîlu) MU.MÍŠ nadin*	3 to the ...... priests and the (temple) servants was given.
4 28⅓ [*pi*] 4½ *ḳa Marduk-zir-ib-ni*	4 28⅓ pi 4½ ka Mardukziribni,

5 *ina mi-šil ûmu* 15 *kam arka ûmu ša araḫ Simanu i-ṭir*	5 in the middle (of the month) on the 15th day after the first day of the month Simanu, paid.
6 75 [*pi*] *Šamaš-iṭi-ir ina tal-lak ûmu* 15 *kam arka ûmu*	6 75 pi Shamashetêr, at the end of the 15th day after the first day
7 *ša araḫ Nisannu* (*amilu*) *mu-tu i-ṭir*	7 of the month Nisannu (to) the...... man, paid.
8 160 + (This line is erased, the traces correspond to line 11, hence probably misplaced.)	
9 15 [*pi*] *Bil-ubulli-iṭ apal* (*amilu*) *pa-ši-ki*	9 15 pi Beluballit, the son of the......,
10 *u Balaṭ-su ana ili Kudurru*	10 and Balatsu for Kudurru (paid).
11 196 [*pi*] *Nabû-zir-gal-lim*	11 196 pi Nabûzirgallim
12 *ûmu* 15 *kam ma-ak-ka-su u ṣil-li i-ṭir*	12 on the 15th day as taxes and rent(?) paid.
13 *napḫaru* 75½ [*pi*] *ili Šamaš-iṭi-ir*	13 Altogether 75½ pi were received from Shamashetêr.
14 5 [*gur*] *ŠE.BAR ša Šamaš-iṭi-ir*	14 5 gur of grain, which Shamashetêr
15 *ša* (*amilu*) *man-di di ina bît ili*	15 for the measurer in the temple of the god (gave),
16 *araḫ Adaru ûmu* 13 *kam šattu* 8 *kam*	16 in the month Adaru, on the 13th day, in the 8th year.
17 3 ...... *ḫar*(?)*-ra-šu ša* (*amilu*) *man-di-di*	17 3 ...... is the (wages) of the measurer.
18 1 *g*[*ur*] *ki-is-ki-*[*ru*] *ša araḫ Nisannu*	18 1 gur is sustenance for the month Nisannu.
19 19 [*pi*] *Balaṭ-su* (*amilu*) *ri'u Musallim-apla*	19 19 pi Balatsu, the shepherd, (and) Musallimapla (paid).
20 35 [*pi*] .... *i-ṭir*	20 35 pi........................paid.

The purport of this tablet is given in the first three lines. It is a list of the debts or tithes that were paid to the priests and temple servants. All these amounts were paid at various dates, but before the end of the month Nisannu of the 9th year. There Mardukziribni pays in the middle of Simanu of the previous year; Shamashetêr has just 15 days to spare for his 75 pi, and 47 days for his 5 gur. Line 13 seems to be a repetition of line 6, and in the 13th line half of a pi has even been added to Shamashetêr's quota. Lines 17 and 18 give the amounts of grain paid to the measurers for their work and their keep.

NO. 9.

OBVERSE.

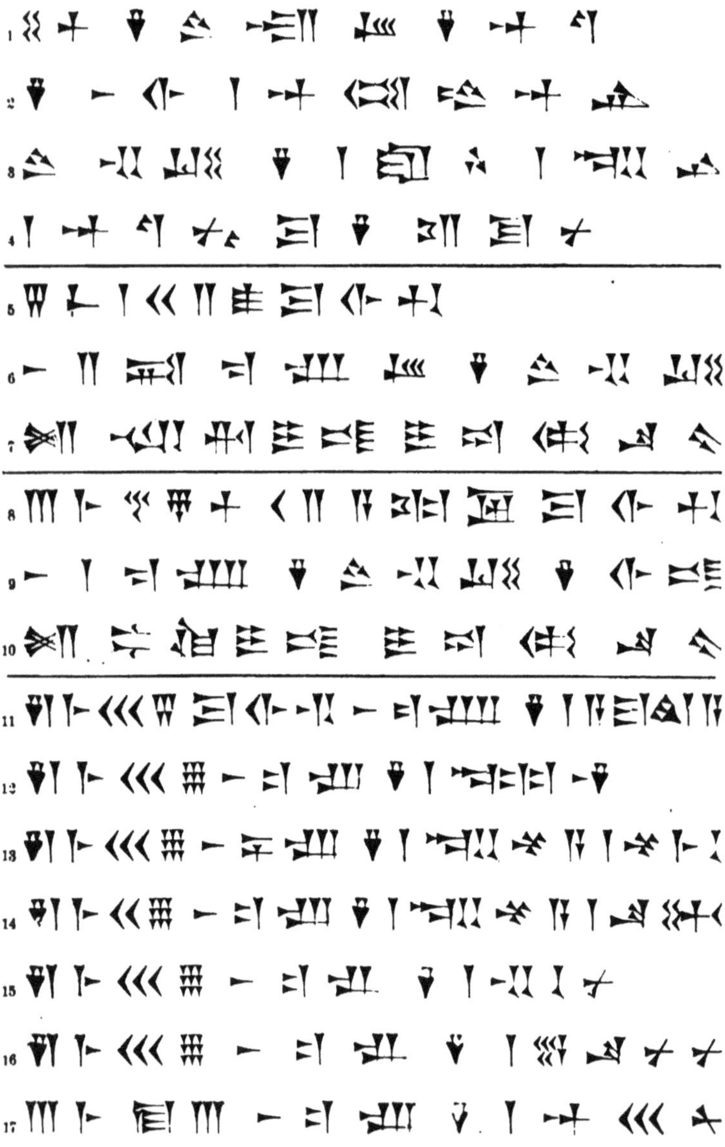

REVERSE.

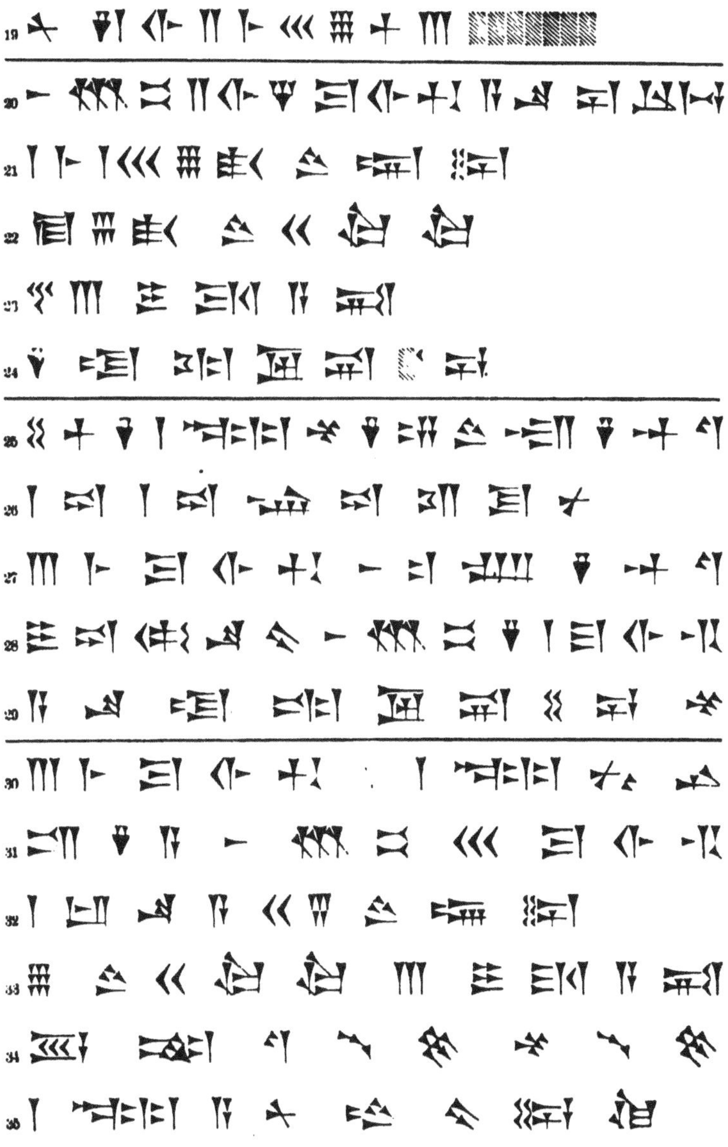

Tablet gray, very hard, surface glazed; 1¾×3 inches. The signs are plainly made. Numerous dividing lines separate the various sentences. The upper, lower, and left edges are not written upon. The right edge contains a few signs of prolonged lines.

1 *ŠÍ.BAR ša (amilu) irriši ša Šamaš*	**1 Grain belonging to the gardeners of Shamash,**
2 *ša ina pâni Marduk-šar-an-ni*	**2 which is at the disposal of Marduk-sharanni,**
3 *(amilu) bil piḫâti ša Ra-tar Bil-ibni*	**3 the prefect, which Ratar, Belibni,**
4 *Šamaš-zir-iḳî-ša iš-šu-nu*	**4 (and) Shamashziriḳisha, brought.**
5 582 *pi ma-ši-ḫu*	**5 582 measures, the size of a pi,**
6 *ina* 2 *ta ilippi ša (amilu) bil piḫâti*	**6 in two ships, belonging to the prefect, (they brought).**
7 *ḫarrânu maḫ-ri-i-tum i-du ul na-din*	**7 In the first business transaction he did not pay freight money.**
8 347½ [*pi*] 12 [*ḳa*] *a-ka-lu ma-ši-ḫu*	**8 347½ pi 12 ka, measures of food,**
9 *ina* 1 *ilippi ša (amilu) bil piḫâti ša pâni-tum*	**9 in one ship belonging to the prefect, (they brought); this is at his disposal.**
10 *ḫarrânu ar-ki-i-tum i-du ul na-din*	**10 In the second business transaction he did not pay freight money.**
11 435 *ma-ši-ḫu ina ilippi ša A-id-a*	**11 435 measures in the ship of Aïda (they brought);**
12 439 *ina ilippi ša Nabû-ițir*	**12 439 in the ship of Nabûetèr;**
13 439 *ina ilippi ša Bil-iddin apal Mu-mi-šu*	**13 439 in the ship of Beliddin, the son of Mumeshu;**
14 429 *ina ilippi ša Bil-iddin apal Na-ṣir*	**14 429 in the ship of Beliddin, the son of Nasir;**
15 439 *ina ilippi ša Bil-šu-nu*	**15 439 in the ship of Belshunu;**
16 439 *ina ilippi ša Iddin-na-nu-nu*	**16 439 in the ship of Iddinnanunu;**
17 363 *ina ilippi ša Sin-uṣur*	**17 363 in the ship of Sinusur;**
18 386 *mašiḫu (ilu)* ......*si-su*	**18 386 measures ......sisu (brought).**
19 *napḫaru* 4239½ [*pi*] 3 [*ḳa*]	**19 Total 4239½ pi 3 ka ....**
20 *ina lib-bi* 2004 *ma-ši-ḫu a-na si-kab*	**20 Thereof 2004 measures are for......;**
21 199 *mašiḫu (amilu) dup-sar*	**21 199 measures (for) the scribe;**
22 66 *mašiḫu (amilu) man-di-di*	**22 66 measures (for) the measurer;**
23 43 *i-da-a-ta*	**23 43 (measures) are the freight moneys**
24 *ša abû ku-lu-uš-[š]i-i*	**24 of the chief ....**
25 *ŠÍ.BAR ša Nabû-šum-iškun-un (amilu) irrišu ša Šamaš*	**25 The grain belonging to Nabûshum-ishkun, the gardener of Shamash,**
26 *Ukin Du-muk-ukin iš-šu-nu*	**26 Ukin (and) Dumukukin brought.**
27 300 *ma-ši-ḫu ina ilippi ša Šamaš*	**27 300 measures in the ship of Shamash (he brought).**
28 *i-du ul na-din ina lib-bi ša* 1 *ma-ši-ḫu*	**28 Freight money he did not pay. Thereof (however) 1 measure**

29 *a na abû ka-lu-uš-ši-i iddin*	29 to the chief .... he gave.
30 300 *ma-ši-ḫu ša Nabû-zir-ibni*	30 300 measures belonging to Nabûzir-ibni
31 *iš-ša-a ina lib-bi* 30 *ma-ši-ḫu*	31 were brought. Thereof 30 measures
32 *Ib-na-a* 25 (*amîlu*) *dup-sar*	32 Ibnâ (received); 25. the scribe;
33 9 (*amêlu*) *man-di-di* 3 *i-da-a-ta*	32 9 the measurer; 3 for freightage.
34 *araḫ Abû ûmu* 9 *kam šattu* 9 *kam*	34 In the month Abu, on the 9th day, in the 9th year of
35 *Nabû-apal-uṣur šar Babili(ki)*	35 Nabopolassar, King of Babylon,

Mardukaharrâni, the prefect of the province, has purchased a large quantity of grain from the gardeners of the temple of Shamash. This grain is to be freighted to him by water. Batar, Belibni, and Shamashzirikisha are selected to transport the grain. They make use of 10 ships. Three of these belong to the prefect, consequently he has to pay no freightage for these, but for the remaining 7 ships his freightage amounts to 43 measures. It is interesting to note that the total given in line 19, is 59 pi 9 ka below the actual amount: evidently the scribe was no expert mathematician. From line 20—24 the disbursements of the prefect are recorded. It is interesting also to note what wages or commission were given to the scribe and to him that measured the grain. The scribe performs intellectual labor, he therefore receives three times as much as the mere measurer. After all deductions the prefect has remaining 2186¼ pi 12 ka.

Lines 25—29 contain the account of Nabûshumishkun; and lines 30—33 that of Nabûziribni. The former spends only one measure for freightage; while the latter spends the disproportionate sum of 67 measures, though each receives 300 measures. Money seems to have been banished entirely from all these transactions, each man is paid in grain, and willingly accepts it.

As there are three accounts made out on this one tablet, I think it the most likely supposition to assume that it was made out for the gardeners of the temple, and was kept in the temple archives at Sippara.

NO. 10.

OBVERSE.

REVERSE.

Tablet brown; 1×2½ inches. The obverse is well preserved, with the exception of the right hand lower corner, which is blurred; the traces of the king's name are, however, certain. Line 10 of the reverse is badly effaced.

1 12 *ma-ši-ḫu ina ḳâtâ Nabû-gud-i-a*	1 12 measures from the hands of Nabûgudea,
2 *ina mi-di-ti ša suluppu*	2 in the measuring of the dates,
3 *ina lib-bi i-mit-tu ša šattu 9 kam*	3 in addition to the dates still on the tree, of the 9th year,
4 *ša ina pân Nabû-šum-iddin apal-šu [ša]*	4 which he was to receive of Nabûshumiddin, the son of
5 *Nabû-na'id ul i-ṭ[ir]*	5 Nabûna'id, he did not receive.
6 *araḫ Kisilimu ûmu 16 kam šattu 9 kam Nabû-apal-uṣur*	6 In the month Kisilimu, on the 16th day, in the 9th year of Nabopolassar.
7 20 *ma-ši-ḫu ša ma-ak-ka-su*	7 20 measures for taxes;
8 85 *mašiḫu* 3 [*ḳa*] *Nabû-tab-ni-ni*	8 85 measures 3 ka Nabûtabniri,
9 5 *mašiḫu* 3 *ḳa Iṭi-ir-Bil*	9 5 measures 3 ka Etêrbel,
10 (*amilu*) *šikaru*	10 the wine ...., (paid);
11 93 *mašiḫu* 3 *ḳa ina pân Bil-apal-iddin*	11 93 measures 3 ka were received of Belapaliddin.

12 *napḫaru* 204 *ma-ši-ḫu Din-na-a*	12 Total: 204 measures, Dinnâ,
13 *i-mit-ti i-ṭir*	13 of dates still on the tree, received.

This tablet seems to be a memorandum kept in the business house of Dinnâ. Nabû-gudea owed Dinnâ twelve measures of dates, which he ought to have paid in the harvest; and Nabûshumiddin owed him the crop of dates that were unripe at the first picking. Neither of these debts was honored. But Dinnâ did receive the 204 measures that were due him from other creditors. According to Peiser a *mašihu* is equal to 9 *ḳa*; hence the fifth sign in line 8 must be taken as 3 instead of ⅓, in order to make the total 204 measures.

NO. 11.

OBVERSE.

REVERSE.

Tablet brown; 1¼×2 inches, rectangular. The three lowest lines of the obverse are badly damaged. The two right corners of the reverse are destroyed. The clay has crumbled off in some places, rendering decipherment difficult. A straight line on the lower edge divides obverse and reverse.

1 2 *ma-na* ⅔ *ma-na* 5 *šiḳlu kaspi ša-lul-tu*	1 2⅔ mana 5 shekels of money, the third (loan ?)
2 *ša ultu Šamaš šim ṣini*	2 which (he received) from Shamash, namely, the price of the sheep,
3 *ina ili Nabû-mudammi-iḳ*	3 to be received from Nabûmudammik,
4 *apal-šu ša Ša-Nabû-šu-u mâr (amilu) ri'u*	4 the son of Shanabûshû, the son of the shepherd.
5 *ina araḫ Adaru [ûmu] 1 a-na Šamaš*	5 In the month Adaru, on the first day, to Shamash
6. *i-nam-din*	6 he will give (the money).
7 *ina manzazu ša Bil-uṣur (amilu) šangu Marduk*	7 In the presence of Belusur, the priest of Marduk;
8 *Mi-nu-u-a-na-Bil mâr*	8 Minûanabel, the son of............,
9 *apal Nûr-Marduk Bil-ib-ni*	9 the son of Nûrmarduk; Belibni,
10 *apal (amilu) šangu Sip-par(ki) Šamaš-nûr-ibni*	10 the son of the priest of Sippara; Shamashnûribni,
11 *apal Dan-ni-dan-a Kudurru apal ri'u sîsi*	11 the son of Dunnidana; Kudurru, the horse herdsman;
12 *u (amilu) dupsar Bil-ukin apal (amilu) šakin in-bu-šu*	12 and the scribe Belukin, the son of the overseer of his fruit (?).
13 *Sip-par(ki) araḫ Nisannu ûmu 12 kam*	13 Sippara, in the month Nisannu, on the 12th day,
14 *šattu 12 kam Nabû-apal-uṣur*	14 in the 12th year of Nabopolassar,
15 *šar Babili(ki)*	15 King of Babylon.

The temple of the sun-god at Sippara had sold Nabûmudammik 2⅔ mana 5 shekels' worth of sheep. But the latter had not paid. He therefore makes out this promissory note, stating that he will pay the money on the first day of Adaru (March). As the tablet mentions no interest, Nabûmudammik seems to have had the use of the money up to that date free.

NO. 12.

OBVERSE.

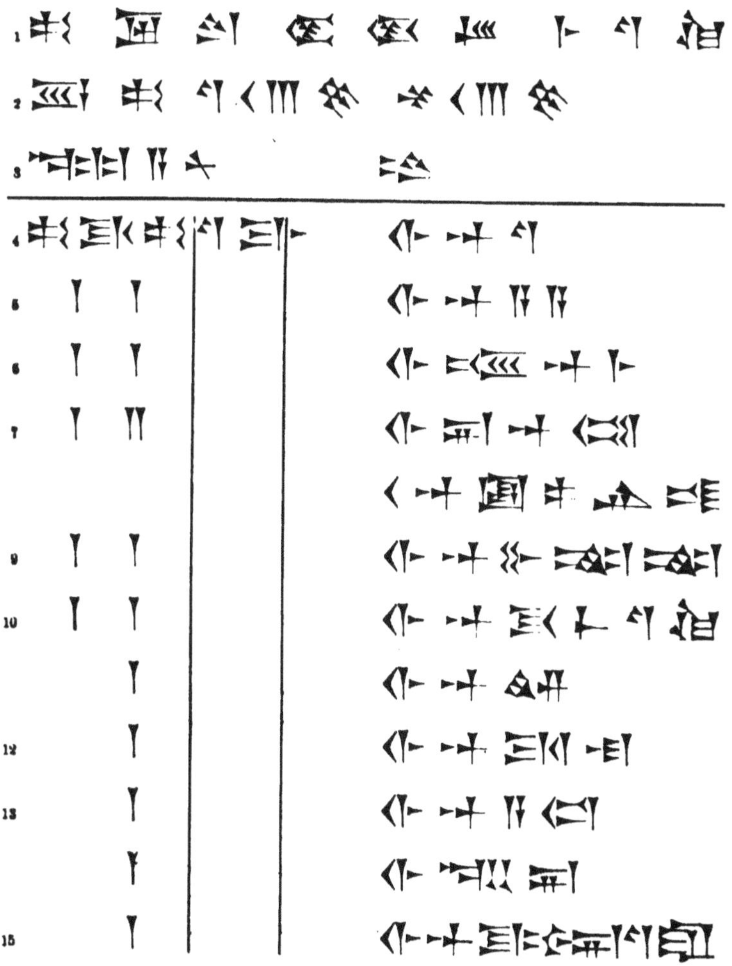

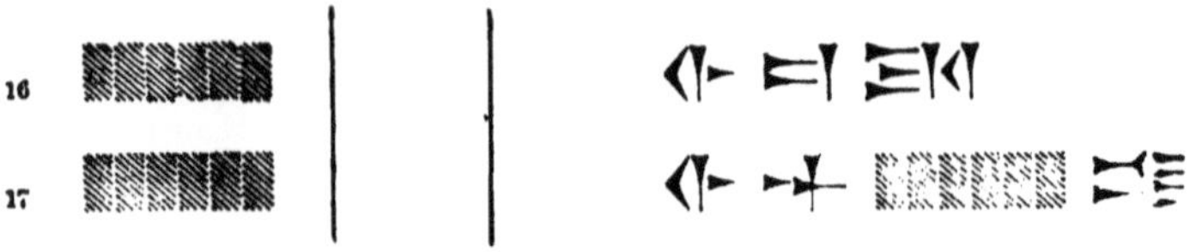

Lines 18 and 19 are effaced, beyond this there seem to be no more lines.

Tablet of a mauve color; 1⅞×3¼ inches. The bottom is totally effaced, the left corner particularly. The reverse seems to have contained no writing, but as the upper part is gone there may have been a few lines there. The signs are roughly made.

1 *alpu LU.NITA niḳî Sip-par(ki)*	1 **Cattle (and) sheep; the sacrifices at Sippara.**
2 *araḫ Airu ûmu 13 kam šattu 13 kam*	2 **In the month Airu, on the 13th day, in the 13th year of**
3 *Nabû-apal-uṣur šarru*	3 **Nabopolassar, the King.**
4 *alpu ŠU.U alpu TU.ḲAL pân (ilu) Šamaš*	4 **A ...... cattle, and a ...... cattle for Shamash;**
5 1 [*alpu ŠU.U*] 1 [*alpu TU.ḲAL*] *pân (ilu) Ai*	5 **one ..... , one ...... for the god Ai;**
6 1 ["] 1 ["] *pân šubti (?) (ilu) ME*	6 **one ......, one ...... for the dewelling of the god Me;**
7 1 ["] 2 ["] *pân bîti (ilu) Marduk*	7 **one ......, two ...... for the temple of Marduk**
8 *u (ilu) Zar-pa-ni-tum*	8 **and Zarpanitum;**
9 1 ["] 1 ["] *pân (ilu) Pu-bil-bil*	9 **one ......, one ...... for the god Pubelbel;**
10 ["] 1 ["] *pân (ilu) Bilit Sip-par(ki)*	10 **one ......, one ..... for Belit of Sippara;**
11 1 [*alpu TU.ḲAL*] *pân (ilu) Rammânu*	11 **one ...... for the god Rammân;**
12 1 ["] *pân (ilu) Ša-la*	12 **one ...... for the god Shala;**
13 1 ["] *pân (ilu) A-num*	13 **one ...... for the god Anu;**
14 1 ["] *pân (ilu) Bil*	14 **one ...... for the god Bel;**
15 1 ["] *pân (ilu) Ia ŠAL.Î.PAR.RA*	15 **one ...... for the god Ea ....;**
16 ...... *pân GIŠ.DA*	16 **...... for ....;**
19 ...... *pân (ilu) [A-nu-ni]-tum*	17 **...... for the goddess (Anuni)tum.**
18 and 19 destroyed.	

This interesting tablet gives us the list of offerings presented to each of the gods in the great temple of the sun-god at Sippara on the 13th day of the month Airu (May), in the 13th year of Nabopolassar. The headings of two columns are given in line 4, and lines are drawn, just as we do to-day in our ledgers. The priest evidently kept a careful account for each day. Other lists of the same character are Nos. 17, 26, etc., to be published in Part III.

NO. 13.

OBVERSE.

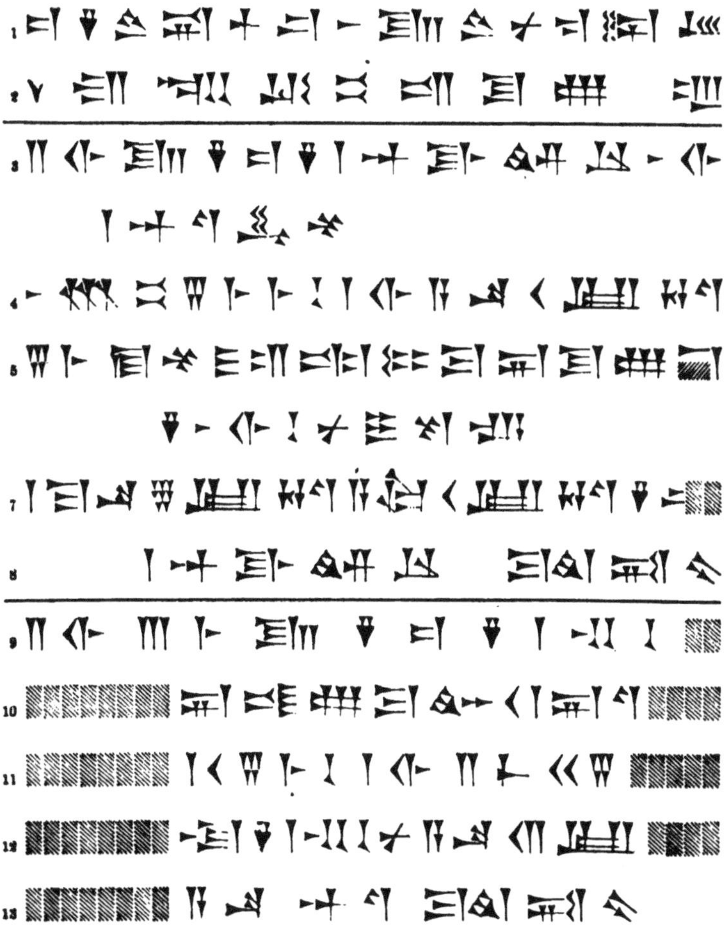

REVERSE.

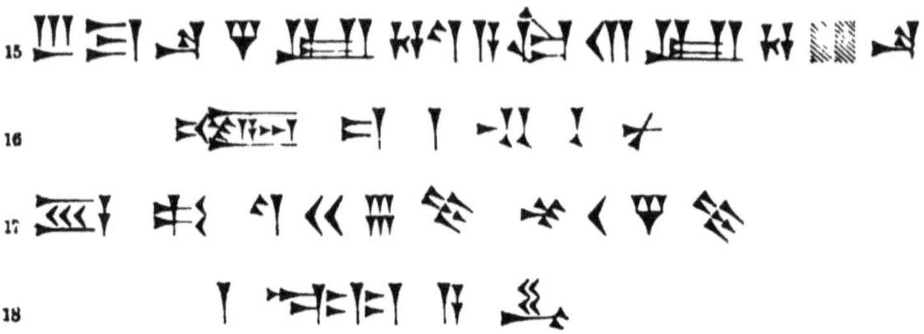

Tablet brown; $1\frac{5}{8}\times2\frac{1}{4}$ inches. Both lower corners of the obverse are broken off. The upper right portion of the reverse is glued on. Above line 18 the numeral for 14 is written, and above line 17, that for 27. These figures, however, can have no meaning here. Two straight lines divide the text, as indicated.

1 *kitû ša (amilu) uš-par kitû ina ḳâtâ (amilu) nu-giš-šar(miš)*	1 Linnen of the weaver. Linnen into the hands of the stewarts
2 *ša alû Bil-iḳ-bi iš-šu-u duppa*	2 of the city Belikbi, he brought for a receipt (?).
3 2000 *ḳat ša kitû ša Bil-na'id ina pân Šamaš-aḫî-iddin*	3 2000 kat of linnen, which Belna'id is to receive from Shamashahiddin;
4 *ina lib-bi* 500 *mi-šu* 1000 [*ḳat*] *a-na* 10 *šiḳlu kaspi*	4 thereof 500 meshu, 1000 kat for 10 shekels of money,
5 500 [*mi-šu*] *ku-mu* 3 *gur suluppu i-šu-u-ma*	5 500 meshu for 3 gur of dates was the sum(?)
6 *ša ina pâni-šu-nu i-ṭi-ṭir*	6 that he paid to them.
7 1 *ma-na* 8 *šiḳlu a-di* 10 *šiḳlu kaspi ša ki*[*tû*]	7 One mana 8 shekels, in addition to the 10 shekels of money (paid) for the linnen,
8 *Bil-na'id il-ta-din*	8 Belna'id gave.
9 2300 *ḳat ša kitû ša Bil-šu-*[*nu*]	9 2300 kat of linnen, which Belshunu
10 .... *bil-tum u-ba-' u Í-tu-*......	10 .... demanded, and Etu.......;
11 [*ina lib-bi* 10]75 *mi-šu* 1225 [*ḳat*]	11 thereof 1075 meshu, 1225 kat,
12 ....*-la ša Bil-šu-nu a-na* 12 *šiḳlu* [*kaspi*]	12 .... which Belshunu for 12 shekels of money
13 .... *a-na Šamaš il-ta-din*	13 (bought), to Shamash he gave.
14 500 [*mi-šu*] *pu-ut zilli ša Šu-la-a a-na šu* ...... *Bil-šu-nu*	14 500 meshu for the joint possession of Shulâ, for ...., Belshunu (acquired);
15 ⅓ *ma-na* 4 *šiḳlu kaspi a-di* 12 *šiḳlu kas*[*pi a*]*-na*	15 ⅓ mana 4 shekels of money, in addition to the 12 shekels of money, for
16 *šîm kitî Bil-šu-nu* [*il-ta-din*]	16 the price of the linnen Belshunu (paid).

17 *araḫ Airu ûmu 26 kam šattu 14 kam*	17 In the month Airu, on the 26th day in the 14th year of
18 *Nabû-apal-uṣur*	18 Nabopolassar.

A weaver brought a certain amount of woven linnen to the stewarts or governors of the city Belikbi. This the latter were to dispose of according to contract. Therefore Belna'id gets 2000 kat. It seems that Shamashahiddin must have been the weaver mentioned in line 1. Of these 2000, 1500 (if we make a *mi-šu* equal to a *ḳat* in value) cost 10 shekels, and the remaining 500, 3 gur of dates. But to this amount must be added the 8 shekels that Belna'id had already paid, perhaps as earnest money.

Then there were 2300 kat, which fell to the share of Belshunu. The text of lines 10, 11, and 12 is so fragmentary that we can only guess how this linnen was paid for. These 2300 kat were divided into 1075 meshu and 1225 kat, for which Belshunu paid 12 shekels into the treasury of the temple of Shamash. Now 500 of these meshu Belshunu seems to have acquired together with Shulá. The above mentioned 12 shekels were probably the commission of the temple. The actual price Belshunu paid for the linnen was ½ mana 4 shekels, in addition to the 12 shekels commission. Hence Belshunu paid altogether 36 shekels for 2300 kat of linnen, while Belna'id paid for 2000 kat 18 shekels and 3 gur of dates, or about half as much. The latter must therefore have known how to drive a bargain, or must have bought much inferior linnen.

This tablet is probably dated at the city of Belikbi, some rich man, who called the city he founded by this name. See No. 7 of this part.

NO. 14.

OBVERSE.

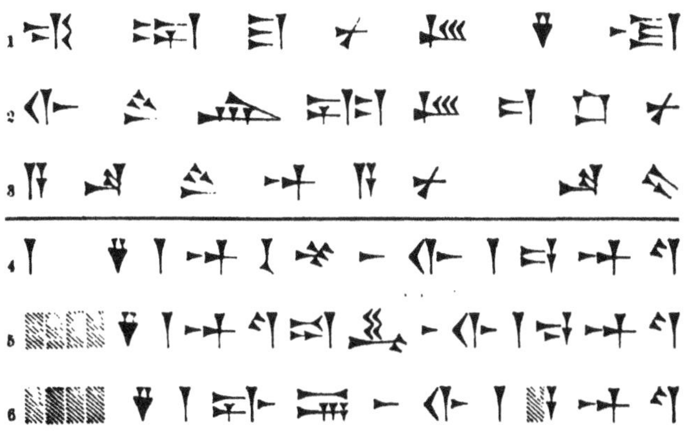

8 

REVERSE.

Tablet shading from light to dark gray; 1¼+2 inches. A straight line is drawn below the 3rd line. The obverse is badly damaged, the lower left corner is completely destroyed. A break occurs in the middle of the upper edge. The right side shows the marks of the thumb as the scribe held the tablet while writing upon it. The upper and left edges are free of writing. A large space at the end is unused.

1 *alpu um-ma-nu(miš) ša la*	1 Cattle, in great numbers, which
2 *pân (amîlu) ir-riš (miš) (iṣu) si-nu*	2 by the gardeners of the ....,
3 *a-na (amilu) [šangu] (ilu) A-nu na-din*	3 were given to the (priests of) the god Anu.
4 *ištin ša Marduk-iddin ina pân Nûr-Šamaš*	4 One (head of cattle), which Mardukiddin has received from Nûrshamash;
5 ...... *ša Šamaš-ukin-aḫî ina pân Nûr-Šamaš*	5 ......, which Shamashukinahi has received from Nûrshamash;
6 ...... *ša Mar-duk ina pân [Nû]r-Šamaš*	6 ......, which Marduk has received from Nûrshamash (and)
7 *Man-nu-di-i-Nabû*	7 Mannudînabû,
8 *[araḫ] Abu ûmu 22 kam*	8 In the month Abu, on the 22nd day,
9 *šattu 17 kam*	9 in the 17th year of
10 *Nabu-apal-uṣur šar Babili(ki)*	10 Nabopolassar, King of Babylon.

This tablet is a receipt for cattle, probably tithes, received by the priests of the temple of the god Anu. Mardukiddin, Shamashukinahi, and Marduk are the priests, Nûrshamash and Mannudînabû are the tithe-payers.

OBVERSE.

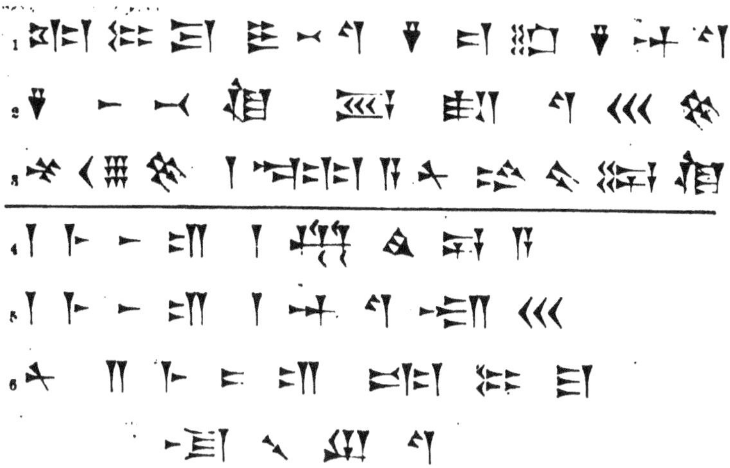

Tablet brown and black; 1×2¼ inches. The four edges contain no writing. The reverse is erased by the scribe, as long crossing lines show. Lines 6 and 7 are very lightly made, and it seems that they just escaped the destructive stylus of the scribe.

1 *sulûpu i-mil-lu ša (iṣu) kiru ša Šamaš*
2 *ina Dil-bat(ki) araḫ Ululu ûmu 30 kam*
3 *šattu 19 kam Nabû-apal-uṣur šar Babili(ki)*
4 101 *gur Uḫ-ḫi-e-a*
5 101 *gur Šamaš-iri-iš*
6 *napḫaru* 202 *gur sulûpu*
7 *la gam-ru-tu*

1 Dates, still hanging on the tree, of the garden of Shamash,
2 at Dilbat. In the month Ululu, on the 30th day,
3 in the 19th year of Nabopolassar, King of Babylon,
4 101 gur Uhhêa (received);
5 101 gur Shamasherêsh (received);
6 Total 202 gur of dates
7 altogether (were sold).

The tablet explains itself. The temple of Shamash at Dilbat sold 202 measures of dates to two persons; and this is a memorandum of that fact. Dilbat is a place occurring in almost every tablet of Peiser's "Keilschriftliche Acten-Stücke aus Babylonischen Städten."

NO. 46.

OBVERSE.

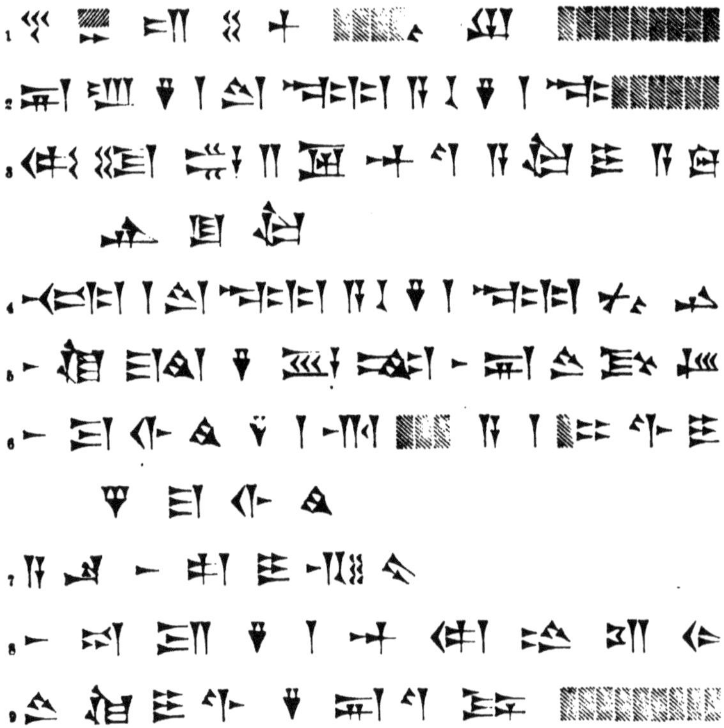

REVERSE.

Tablet dark gray; 1⅞×2¼ inches. The upper edge of the obverse is destroyed, and the surface is marred in various places as is indicated above. The reverse is tolerably well preserved. Edges free of writing, except that the name or the river in line 3, is upon the right edge. The signs are large and plain.

1 44 *gur ŠÍ.BAR .... ru ......*	1 **44 gur of grain, ...**
2 *Í.DUP ša Arad-Nabû apal-šu ša Nabû- ......*	2 **the amount (?), which Aradnabû, the son of Nabû ......, (in the space)**
3 *ul-tu bâbâni ṣinî Šamaš a-di-i (nâru) Ni-ku-di*	3 **from the two sheep-gates of Shamash to the river Nikudi,**
4 *ina íli Arad-Nabû apal-šu ša Nabû-zir-ibni*	4 **from Aradnabû, the son of Nabûziribni, is to receive.**
5 *ina ki-it ša araḫ [Abu] ina bîti (amîlu) rab (miš)*	5 **At the end of the month Abu, in the house of the chiefs,**
6 *ina ma-ši-ḫi ša Ri-[mut] apal Mi-pi-i 4 ma-ši-ḫi*	6 **according to the measure of Rimut, the son of Mipi, (that is,) 4 measures**
7 *a-na 1 gur i-nam-din*	7 **as one gur, he will give**
8 *ina manzazu ša Nirgal-šar-mil-lit*	8 **in the presence of Nergalsharmillit,**
9 *(amîlu) ki-i-pi ša BIT.TU m?r......*	9 **the guardian of the ......, the son of ......, (and)**
10 *Mu-ši-zib-Marduk (amîlu) šangu Sip-par(ki)*	10 **Mushezibmarduk, the priest of Sippara.**
11 *(amîlu) mu-kin-nu Nabû-zir-lišir apal-šu [ša]*	11 **Witnesses: Nabûzirlishir, the son of**
12 *Balaṭu (amîlu) pa-ši-ki ....*	12 **Balatu, the ......; ....,**
13 *apal-šu ša Šu-la-a apal Iddin-Mar[duk]*	13 **the son of Shulâ, the son of Iddinmarduk;**
14 *Mu-ra-nu apal-šu ša Lu-uṣ-ana-nûri*	14 **Muranu, the son of Lûsananûre,**
15 *apal Ša-na-ši-šu u (amîlu) dupsar Arad-Bíl*	15 **the son of Shanashishu; and the scribe Arudbel,**
16 *apal-šu ša Nabû-aḫî-iddin apal (amîlu) pa-ši-ki*	16 **the son of Nabûahiddin, the son of the ......**
17 *Sip-par(ki) araḫ Nisannu ûmu 25 kam*	17 **Sippara, in the month Nisannu, on the 25th day,**

18 *šattu* 3 *kam Nabû-na'id šar Babili(ki)*	18 in the 3rd year of Nabonidus, King of Babylon.

Aradnabû is to receive 44 gur of grain from his namesake in the month Abu (August), and at a place somewhere between the two gates of the Shamash temple, called the sheep-gates, and the river Nikudi. Here in one of the government agencies, the second Aradnabû (the two are distinguished by the names of their fathers) will measure out the 44 gur, using the measure of a person named Rîmut as a standard. Four of these standard measures shall be considered the equivalent of one gur. At the measuring of the grain Nergalsharmillit and Mushezibmarduk will be present to see that the measuring is done honestly. The contract was made in the month Nisannu (April), and hence had four months to run.

NO. 47.

OBVERSE.

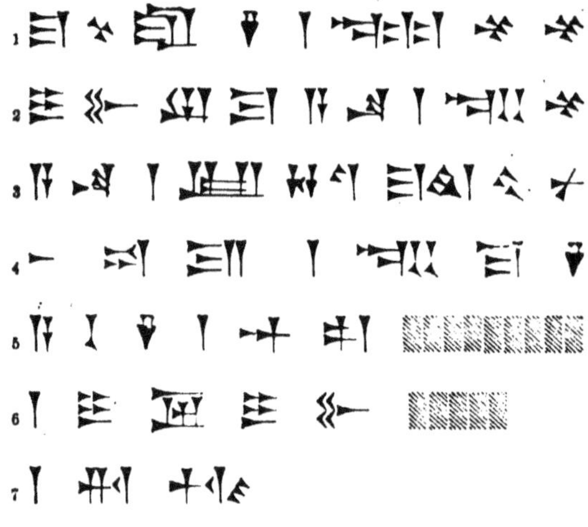

REVERSE.

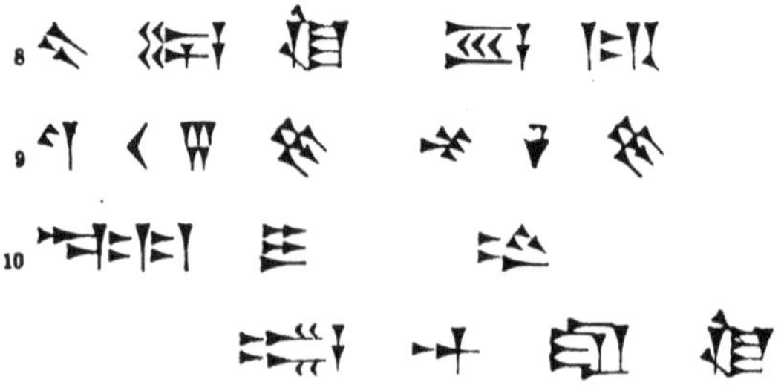

Tablet gray with numerous black spots; $1\frac{1}{4} \times 1\frac{5}{8}$ inches. The lower right corner of the obverse is flattened down, thus destroying part of two witnesses' names. The reverse is perfect.

1 *ma-kur-ru ša Nabû-šum-iddin*	1 The merchandise, which Nabûshum-iddin,
2 *i-bu-ru-ma a-na Bil-iddin*	2 namely the harvest, to Beliddin
3 *a-na* 1 *šiklu kaspi id-din-nu*	3 for one shekel of money gave,
4 *ina manzazu Bil-ikî-ša*	4 In the presence of Belikisha,
5 *apal-šu ša Nirgal*	5 the son of Nergal ......,
6 *I-lu-i-pu-[uš]*	6 Iluïpûsh, (and)
7 *Ri-mut*	7 Rimut.
8 *Babilu(ki) arah Ululu*	8 Babylon, in the month Ululu,
9 *ûmu* 15 *kam šattu* 3 *kam*	9 on the 15th day, in the 3rd year of
10 *Nabû-na'id šar*	10 Nabonidus, King of
11 *Babili(ki)*	11 Babylon.

This tablet is a receipt pure and simple. Nabûshumiddin sold one shekel's worth of produce to Beliddin, and gave him this receipt for his money.

NO. 48.

OBVERSE.

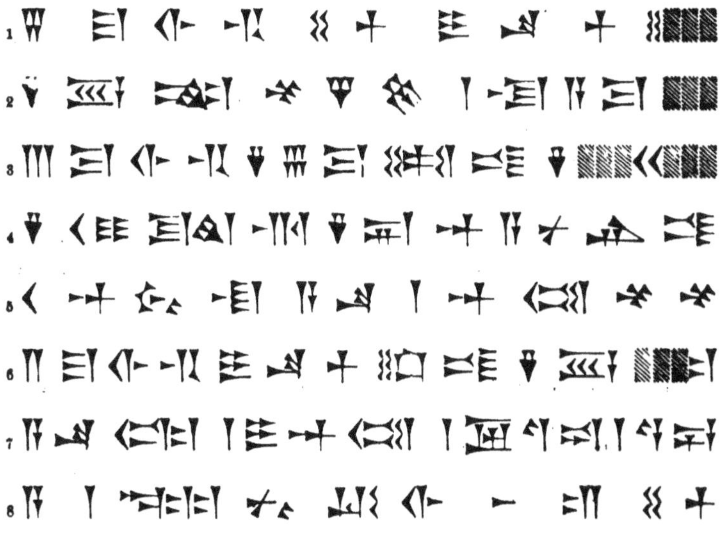

REVERSE.

Tablet light brown; 1⅞×2¼ inches. The clay has crumbled off in numerous places. The right upper corner of the obverse is destroyed, and a large crack divides the upper portion of the reverse, on the right side, from the rest of the tablet. The writing is tolerably distinct. The left and the upper edges are free of writing.

1 5 *ma-ši-ḫu ŠÍ. BAR i-na maš-ša[r-tum]*	1 5 measures of grain at the end
2 *ša araḫ Abu šattu 4 kam La-a-ba-[ši]*	2 of the month Abu, of the 4th year, Labâshi (will give);
3 3 *ma-ši-ḫu ša* 6 *ba-li-tum ša*	3 3 measures with 6 talents of .... (and)
4 *ša* 16 *iṭ(?)-ri ša bîti (ilu) A-nu-ni-tum*	4 with 16 ...... for the temple of the goddess Anunitum
5 *u (ilu) Gu-la a-na Marduk-šum-iddin*	5 and the goddess Gula, to Marduk-shumiddin (he will give).
6 2 *ma-ši-ḫu i-na maš-šar-tum ša araḫ [A]bu*	6 2 measures, at the end of the month Abu,

7 *a-na ili Na'id-Marduk Lu-uṣ-ana-nûr-i*	7 on the account of Na'idmarduk, Lûsananûre,
8 *apal Nabû-zir-gal-lim* 1 *gur ŠÍ.BAR*	8 the son of Nabûzirgallim, (will give). 1 gur of grain,
9 *LU.NITA ki-mi ša ša-lam-ma Gi-mil-u*	9 sheep, wholesome flour (?) Gimillu
10 *ina ḳâtâ Ba-la-ṭu-ma i-nam-din*	10 into the hands of Balatu will give:
11 *Ba-la-ṭu ŠÍ.BAR-šu i-ṭir*	11 Balatu has received his grain.
12 + 2 *pi ŠÍ.BAR a-na ḳu-ur-ru-bu*	12 + 2 pi of grain for the offering
13 *ša a-šu-ḫu*	13 of ....
14 5 *ma-ši-ḫu i-na maš-šar-tum*	14 5 measures at the end
15 *ša araḫ Abu šattu* 4 *kam a-na*	15 of the month Abu, of the 4th year, to
16 *Mu-ra-nu apal Lu-uṣ-ana-nûr-i*	16 Muranu, the son of Lûsananûre, (he will give):
17 *ŠÍ.BAR ina ḳâtâ Šamaš-irba ša bît alpi*	17 the grain is to be received of Shamash-irba at the house of the cattle.
18 *araḫ Nisannu ûmu* 3 *kam šattu* 4 *kam*	18 In the month Nisannu, on the 3rd day, in the 4th year of
19 *Nabû-na'id šar Babili(ki)*	19 Nabonidus, King of Babylon.

This tablet is evidently a statement containing the debts of Labâshi, Lûsananure and Gimillu. Very likely this statement was issued by some agent, through whose hands the merchandise and the money had to pass.

NO. 49.

OBVERSE.

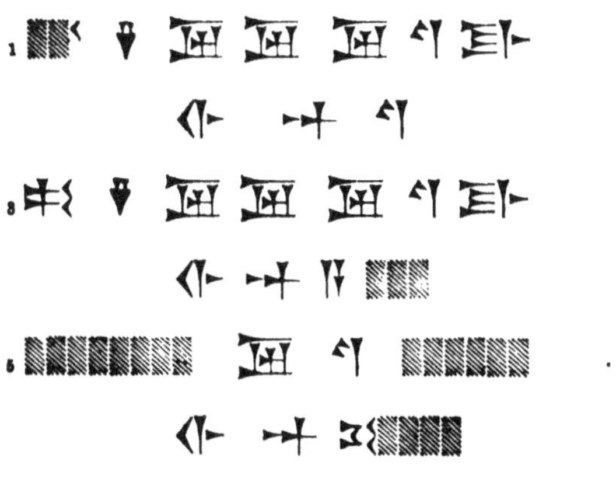

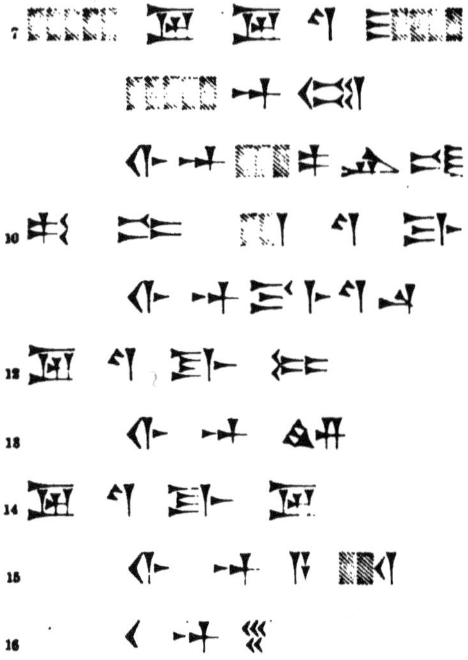

REVERSE.

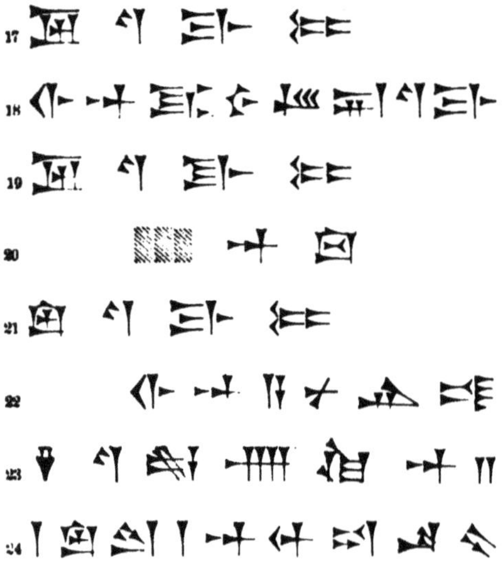

Tablet light brown; 1⅜×2¾ inches. The surface has crumbled away in many places, and thus the tablet is in a very bad condition. The best rendering possible is given below.

1 [*alp*]*u ša ṣinî LU.TU.ḲAL*	1 Cattle, namely .... sheep,
2 *pân* (*ilu*) *Šamaš*	2 for the god Shamash.
3 *alpu ša ṣinî LU.TU.ḲAL*	3 Cattle, namely .... sheep,
4 *pân* (*ilu*) *A*-[*num*]	4 for the god Anu.
5 [*alpu ša ṣinî*] *LU.TU* [*ḲAL*]	5 Cattle, namely .... sheep,
6 *pân* (*ilu*) *Mar*[*duk*]	6 for the god Marduk.
7 [*alpu ša ṣi*]*nî LU.TU.ḲA*[*L*]	7 Cattle, namely .... sheep,
8 [*pân*] (*ilu*) *Marduk*	8 for the god Marduk (and)
9 *pân* (*ilu*) [*Zar*]-*pa-ni-tum*	9 for the goddess Zarpanitum.
10 *alpu ṣu*. .... [*L*]*U.TU.ḲAL*	10 Cattle, namely ....,
11 *pân* (*ilu*) *Bilit-mi-tu-ḳa*	11 for the goddess Belitmetuka.
12 *LU.TU.ḲAL.LUM*	12 ....
13 *pân* (*ilu*) *Rammânu*	13 for the god Rammân.
14 *LU.TU.ḲAL.LU*	14 ....
15 *pân* (*ilu*) *A*-[*nu*]*m*	15 for the god Anu.
16 *u* (*ilu*) *Bil*	16 and the god Bel.
17 *LU.TU.ḲAL.LUM*	17 ....
18 *pân* (*ilu*) *marâti bît TU.ḲAL*	18 for the gods, the daughters of the house of ....
19 *LU.TU.ḲAL.LUM*	19 ....
20 [*pân*] (*ilu*) *GAR*	20 for the god Gar.
21 *LU.TU.ḲAL.LUM*	21 ....
22 *pân* (*ilu*) *A-nu ni-tum*	22 for the goddess Anunitum
23 *ša Sippari*(*ki*) *ilâni šina*	23 of Sippara: two goddesses.
24 1 *LU.NITA Nirgal*(?)-*ukin-na-balaṭu*	24 One sheep Nergalukinnabalatu (gave).
25 1 *alpu u* 3 *ṣinî*	25 One head of cattle and 3 sheep
26 *Nabû-u-ši-zib il-ta-din*	26 Nabûshezib gave.

27 *araḫ Šamna ûmu 22 k[am]*	27 In the month Samna, on the 23rd day,
28 [*šattu*] 4 [*kam*] *Nabû-*[*na'id*]	28 in the 4th year of Nabonidus,
29 [*š*]*ar Babili*(*ki*)	29 King of Babylon.

This tablet gives us a list of the offerings made to the gods at Sippara in the great temple of the sun-god on the 22nd day of the month Samna (November), in the 4th year of Nabonidus. Besides the regular offerings, Nergalukiunabalatu and Nabûshezib seem to have made sacrifices.

The break on the tablet at the end of line 27 shows indistinct traces of the sign *i*, and hence I have placed this tablet among those of Nabonidus, rather than among those of Nabopolassar, to whose reign most of the tablets of this class must be referred.

NO. 50.

OBVERSE.

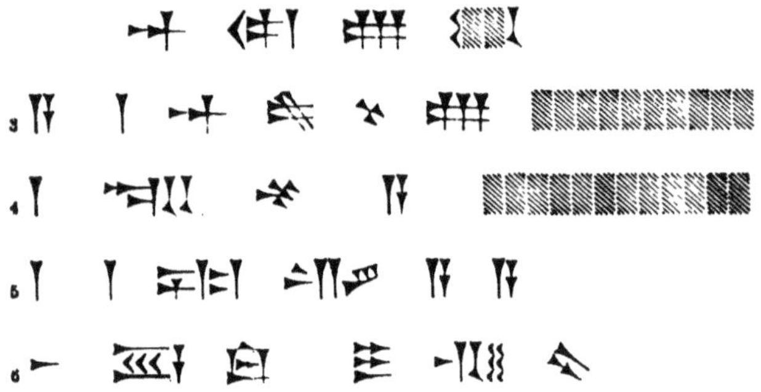

REVERSE.

Tablet light gray; 1¼×1⅜ inches. The first line of the obverse is totally effaced, likewise the upper left corner of the reverse. The tablet, on the whole, is very much damaged.

2	*Nirgal-u-kin*	2	Nergalukin,
3	*apal (ilu) Îllat-u [a-na]*	3	the son of Ellatu, (to)
4	*Bîl-iddin apal*	4	Beliddin, the son of
5	*Sag-gil-ai*	5	Saggilai,
6	*ina araḫ Tašritu i-nam-din*	6	in the month Tashritu, will give.
7	*[(amîlu) mu-ki]n-nu Nirgal-šum-ibni*	7	Witnesses: Nergalshumibni,
8	*[apal-šu-ša] Nabû-šum-iddin apal Arad-Bil*	8	the son of Nabûshumiddin, the son of Aradbel;
9	*Nabû-balaṭ-su iḳ-bi apal-šu ša*	9	Nabûbalatsuikbi, the son of
10	*Marduk-irba apal Iddin-Marduk*	10	Mardukirba, the son of Iddinmarduk:
11	*u (amîlu) dupsar Bîl-iddin apal-šu ša Ki-ṣir-Nabû*	11	and the scribe Beliddin, the son of Kisirnabû.
12	*Babilu(ki) araḫ Airu ûmu 22 kam*	12	Babylon, in the month Airu, on the 22nd day,
13	*šattu 5 kam Nabû-na'id*	13	in the 5th year of Nabonidus,
14	*šar Babili(ki)*	14	King of Babylon.

This tablet is a regular promissory note. Nergaliddin promises to give to Beliddin either money or some commodity in the month Tashritu (October).

NO. 51.

OBVERSE.

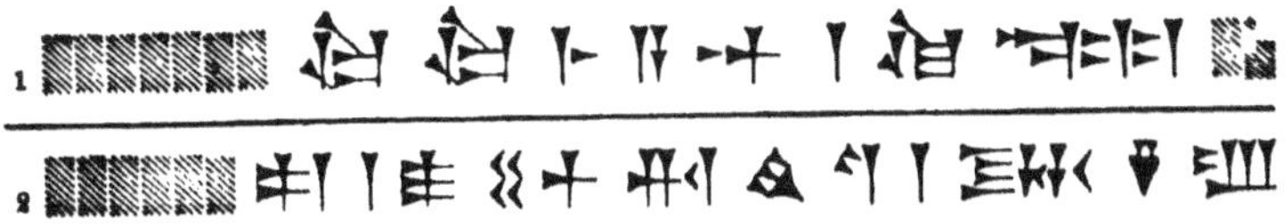

3 

4 

5 *This line is erased by the scribe.*

6 

7 

8 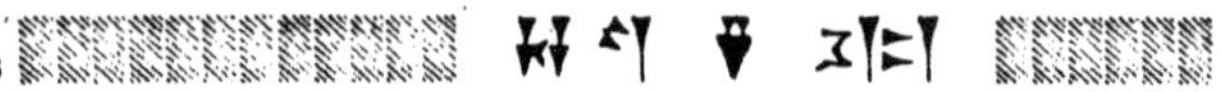

About two lines on the obverse, and two on the reverse are broken off

REVERSE.

13 

14 

15 

16 

17 

18 

19 

Tablet light brown; 1¾×2¼ inches. A fragment All four edges are broken off. The signs are plain and well-made.

1 ....*di-li mi a.an Itti-Nabû-* [*balaṭu*] ....

1 ...... (gur of measured grain ?) 100 each Ittinabûbalatu ....

2 ...... *gur* 1 *pi* ŠÎ BAR *ri-ḫi-tu Piš-ša-dup*	2 ...... gur, 1 pi of grain, the remainder, Pishshadup,
3 *a-di araḫ Ṭibitu šattu* 6 *kam Nabû-na'id šarru*	3 until the month Tebitu of the 6th year of Nabonidus the King, (will give).
4 30 *gur ultu bît bûšu araḫ Ṭibitu šattu* 6 [*kam*]	4 30 gur from the storehouse in the month Tebitu of the 6th year, (he will give).

Line 5 is erased.

6 28 *gur* 3 *pi ina bît bûšu araḫ*	6 28 gur 3 pi into the storehouse, in the month ...... (he will deliver).
7 ...... *gur ina ḳâtâ Nabû-šum-iddin*	7 ...... gur from the hands of Nabû-shumiddin (he will receive).
8 ...... *kaspu ša ka*	8 ...... money of ....

Four or more lines are broken off.

13 ...... *Nabû-gab-zu a-di ûmu*	13 ...... Nabûgabzu until the .... day ....
14 ...... *ki-mi-mi bîti Šapik-zir*	14 ...... sustenance of the house of Shapikzir ....
15 ...... *Ai ana ili pi-i ša Itti-Na[bû-balaṭu]*	15 ...... Ai, according to the word of Ittinabûbalatu, (took).
16 ......*-šu* ŠÎ BAR*-šu Arad-Gula a-na ili pi-i ša Itti-[Nabû-balaṭu]*	16 .. ... his ...... of his grain Arad-gula according to the word of Ittinabûbalatu (took).
17 [*araḫ*] *Nisannu ûmu* 7 *kam šattu* 7 *k[am]*	17 In the month Nisannu, on the 7th day, in the 7th year of
18 [*Nab*]*û-na'id šar Babili* [(*ki*)] ...... *ša*	18 Nabû-na'id, King of Babylon. ... .
19 *tum*	19 ....

The defective condition of this fragment will allow me only to make a supposition in regard to the subject matter of the text. Ittinabûbalatu seems to have been the overseer of some public granary. He is, in the first place, to receive 100 gur each from certain persons, and then he is to mete these out again in the month Tebitu, but in smaller amounts each. Whether the same persons that gave the grain are to receive part of it back, paying the remainder for the use of the storehouse or whether the givers and the receivers are different persons, our fragmentary text does not state. At least, it is certain, according to lines 15 and 16, that Ittinabûbalatu was an authoritative person, and that his word had some weight in the management of the granary.

NO. 52.

OBVERSE.

About one line on the obverse, and one on the reverse are broken off.

REVERSE.

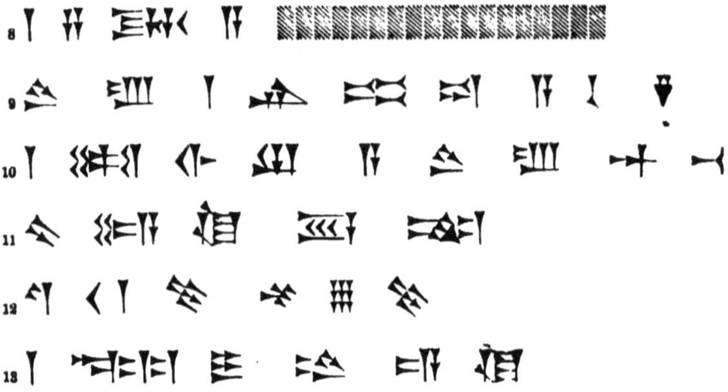

Tablet light gray, a fragment; 1×1⅜ inches. The bottom is broken off, destroying two, possibly more, lines. The signs are plain, though well-worn away.

1 *ina u-an-tim (miš) ša ŠÍ.BAR*
2 *ša Bíl-uballi-iṭ apal-šu ša Din-na-a apal Í-ṭi-ru*
3 *ša ina íli La-a-ba-ši apal-šu ša Balaṭu*

1 Upon the certificates for grain,
2 belonging to Beluballit, the son of Dinnâ, the son of Etéru,
3 which is to be received of Labâshi, the son of Balatu,

4 *apal Sag-gil-ai u Tu-'*	4 the son of Saggillai, and of Tu'.
5 *apal-šu ša Nabû-êṭir apal Ik-b[i]-*	5 the son of Nabûetêr, the son of Ikbi ..,

Two or more lines are destroyed.

8 *Za-kir apal*	8 Zakir, the son of ....
9 (*amîlu*) *dupsar Ni-ku-du apal-šu ša*	9 Scribe: Nikudu, the son of
10 *Li-ši-ru apal* (*amîlu*) *šangu Bil*	10 Lishiru, the son of the priest of Bel.
11 *Babilu(ki) araḫ Abu*	11 Babylon in the month Abu,
12 *ûmu* 11 *kam šattu* 9 *kam*	12 on the 11th day, in the 9th year of
13 *Nabû-na'id šar Babili(ki)*	13 Nabonidus, King of Babylon.

Beluballit has in his possession certificates entitling him to a certain quantity of grain from Labâshi and Tu'. He now proceeds, on the strength of these, to take part of his possessions, and this tablet, duly inscribed with the fact, is then given to the two latter persons.

NO. 53.

OBVERSE.

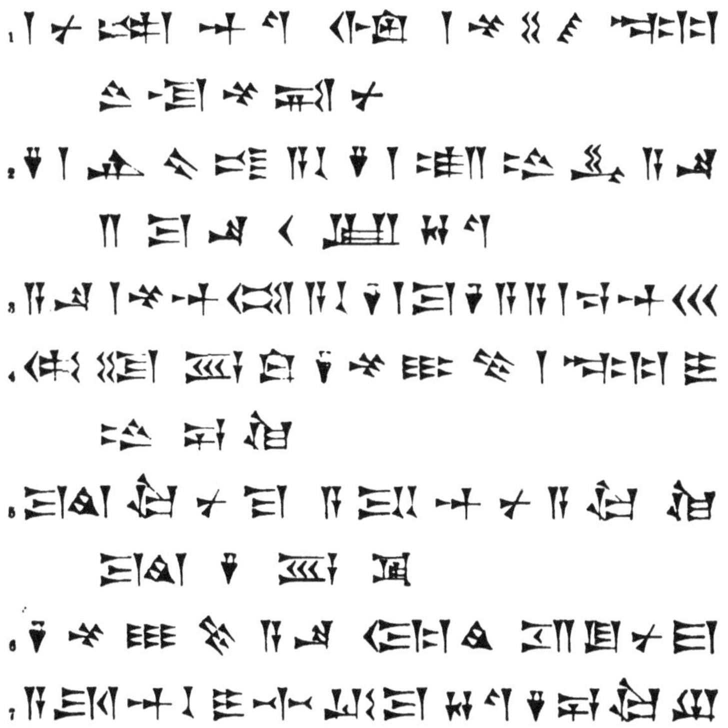

REVERSE.

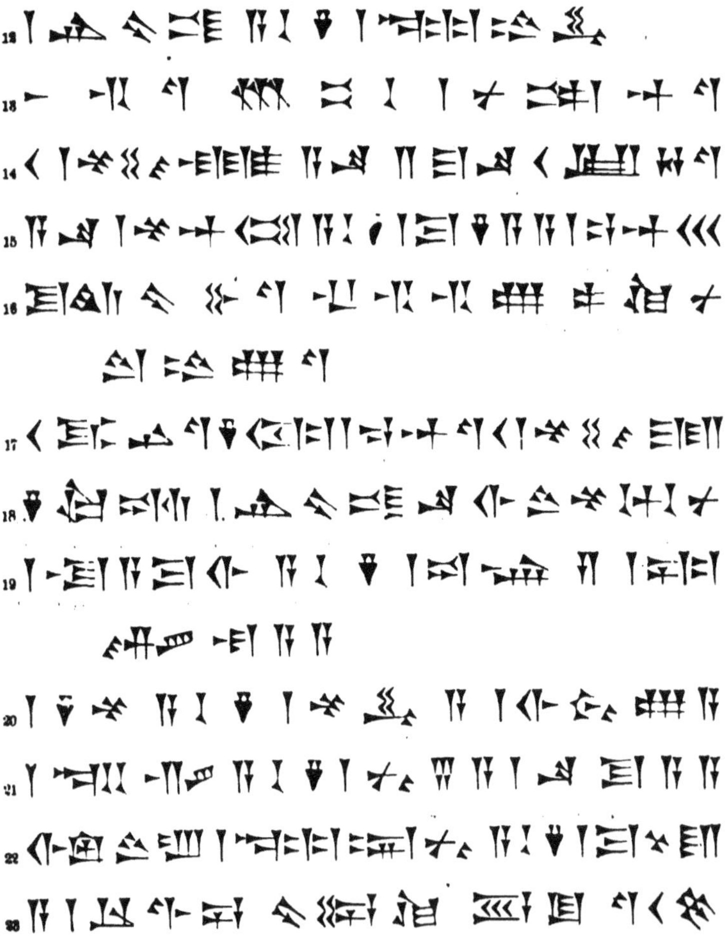

24 

LEFT SIDE.

25 

26 

Tablet dark brown; 1⅞×2⅜ inches. The tablet is in perfect condition, with the exception of the lower part of the left edge, where the signs are very blurred. The right edge is covered by the signs of lines prolonged from obverse and reverse, with the exception of the upper part which is free of wedges, and which contains the number of the tablet.

1 *Nu-ur-Šamaš u Mu-ši-zib-Nabû (amîlu) la-mu-ta-nu*	1 Nurshamash and Mushezibnabû, the servants,
2 *ša Ni-din-tum apal-šu ša Nabû-šar-uṣur a-na 2 ma-na 10 šiḳlu kaspi*	2 whom Nidintum, the son of Nabû-sharusur, for 2 mana 10 shekels of money
3 *a-na Iddin-Marduk apal-šu ša Iḳî-ša-apla apal Nûr-Sin*	3 to Iddinmarduk, the son of Ikishâpla, the son of Nûrsin,
4 *ul-tu araḫ Tašritu ša šattu 8 kam Nabu-na'id šar Babili(ki)*	4 from the month Tashritu of the 8th year of Nabonidus, King of Babylon, on,
5 *id-di-nu-ma a-da-an-nu a-di ki-it ša araḫ Ululu*	5 gave; and the term (of payment) till the end of the month Ululu
6 *ša šattu 9 kam a-na iii iš-ku-nu-ma*	6 of the 9th year on his account be set.
7 *a-da-an-šu i-ti-ik-ma kaspu ša i-ṭi-ru*	7 His term (of payment) had passed away, and the money which he should pay
8 *lâ i-ši Ni-din-tum a-na Iddin-Marduk*	8 there was not. (Then) Nidintum to Iddinmarduk
9 *iḳ-bi um-ma kaspu a-na i-ṭi-ri-ka*	9 said "(Since) money for thy payment (to me)
10 *lâ i-ši Nûr-Šamaš u Mu-ši-zib-Nabû*	10 there is not, Nûrshamash and Mushezibnabû
11 *[a-n]a duppi šîmi gam-ru-tu a-bu-uk*	11 for a tablet of the full price, I will bring; (which tablet shall say)
12 *Ni-din-tum apal-šu ša Nabû-šâr-uṣur*	12 'Nidintum, the son of Nabûsharusur,
13 *ina ḫu-ud lib-bi-šu Nu-ur-Šamaš*	13 of his own free will, Nûrshamash
14 *u Mu-ši-zib-Nabû a-na 2 ma-na 10 šiḳlu kaspi*	14 and Mushezibnabû for 2 mana 10 shekels of money,

15 *a-na Iddin-Marduk apal-šu ša Iḳî-ša-apla apal Nûr-Sin*	15 to Iddinmarduk, the son of Ikishâpla, the son of Nûrsin,
16 *id-din pu-ut si-ḫu-ḫu-u pa-ki-nu arad-šar-u-tu*	16 gave. Against flight, reclaiming by the seller, reclaiming by the king's officer,
17 *u mâr-bûnu-tu ša ili Nûr-Šamaš u Mu-ši-zib-Nabû*	17 and previous adoption, which about Nûrshamash and Mushezibnabû
18 *ša ṭi-il Ni-din-tum na-ši (amilu) mu-kin-nu*	18 might arise, Nidintum will be responsible.'" Witnesses:
19 *La-a-ba-ši apal-šu ša Du-muḳ apal Sag-gil-la-ai*	19 Labâshi, the son of Dumuk, the son of Saggillai;
20 *Šakin-šum apal-šu ša Šum-uṣur apal Ši-gu-u-a*	20 Shakinshum, the son of Shumusur, the son of Shigûa;
21 *Bêl-musallim apal-šu ša Ziri-ia apal Na-šu-ai*	21 Belmusallim, the son of Ziria, the son of Nashuai;
22 *u (amilu) dupsar Nabû-šapik-zir apal-šu ša Ba-laṭ-su*	22 and the scribe Nabûshapikzir, the son of Balatsu,
23 *apal Tuk-pi-i Bâbilu(ki) araḫ Tašritu ûmu 10 kam*	23 the son of Tukpê. Babylon, in the month Tashritu, on the 10th day,
24 *šattu 9 kam Nabû-na'id šar Bâbili(ki)*	24 in the 9th year of Nabonidus, King of Babylon.
25 *ina a-šu-bi ša Î-ba-tum aššati-šu ......*	25 In the presence of Ebatum, the wife of ....,
26 *marat-su ša Marduk-šum-ibni apal Šu-[la-a]*	26 the daughter of Mardukshumibni, the son of Shulâ.

This tablet treats of the sale of two slaves by Nidintum to Iddinmarduk. A contract tablet was at first made, according to which the 2 mana 10 shekels were to be paid at the end of the month Ululu in the 9th year of the reign of Nabonidus. But Iddinmarduk found himself unable to pay at the appointed time. So Nidintum, immediately in the beginning of the succeeding month, has a tablet made, recording the absolute sale of the slaves, and allowing the money to remain as a debt over Iddinmarduk. What interest, if any, the latter is to pay, is not stated here.

NO. 54.

OBVERSE.

1
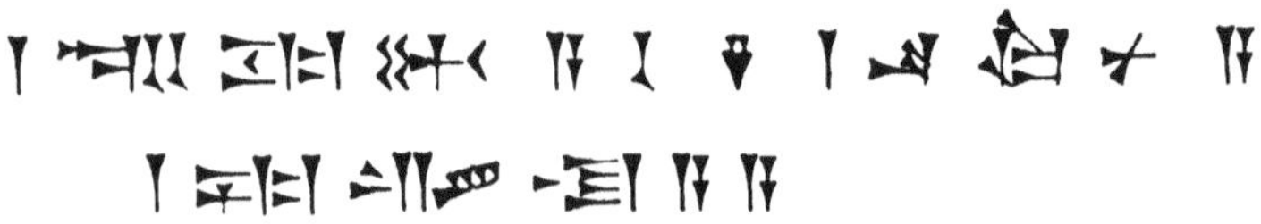

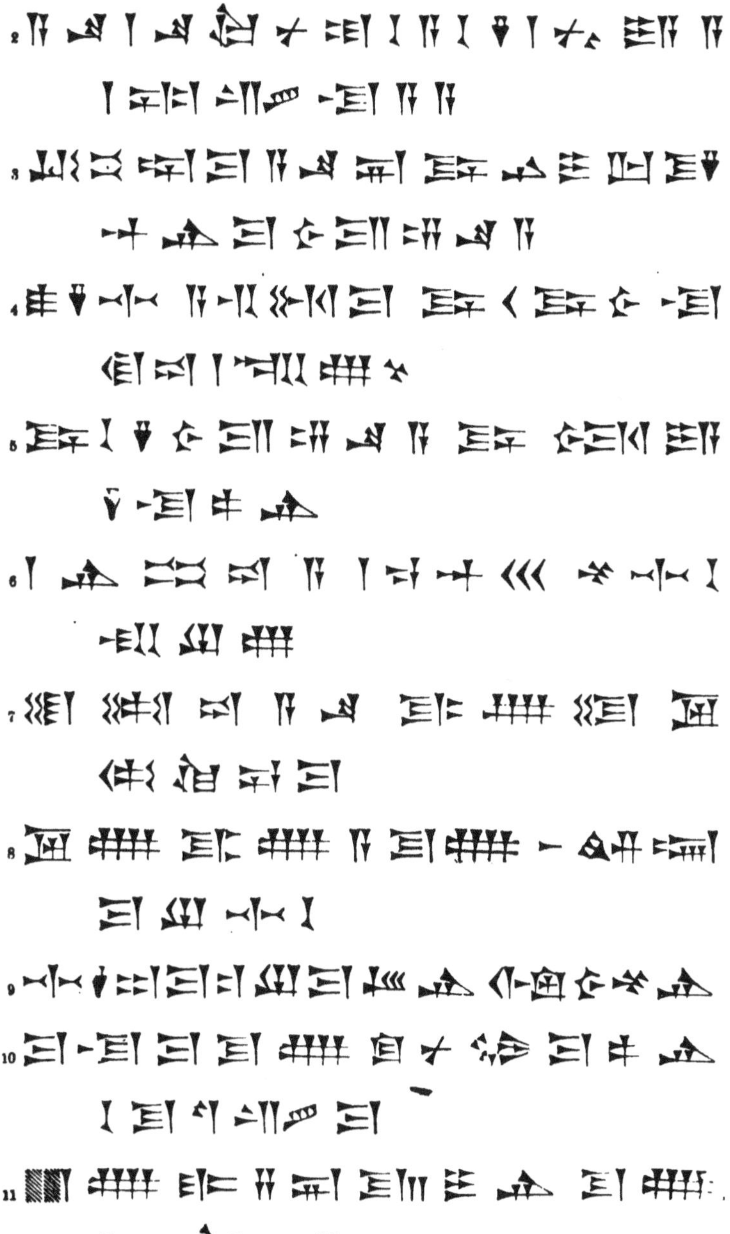

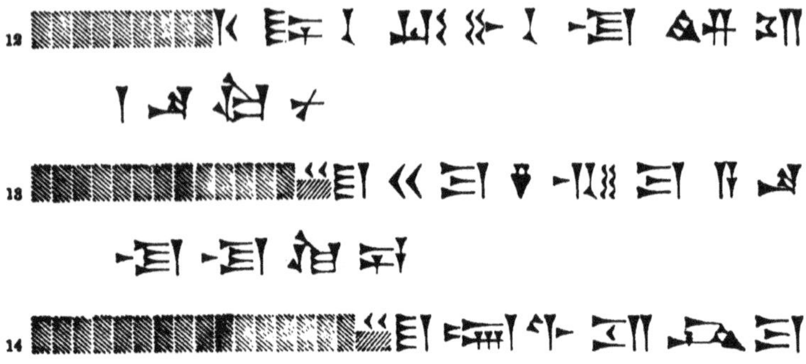

According to my judgment about fifteen lines are broken off here.

REVERSE.

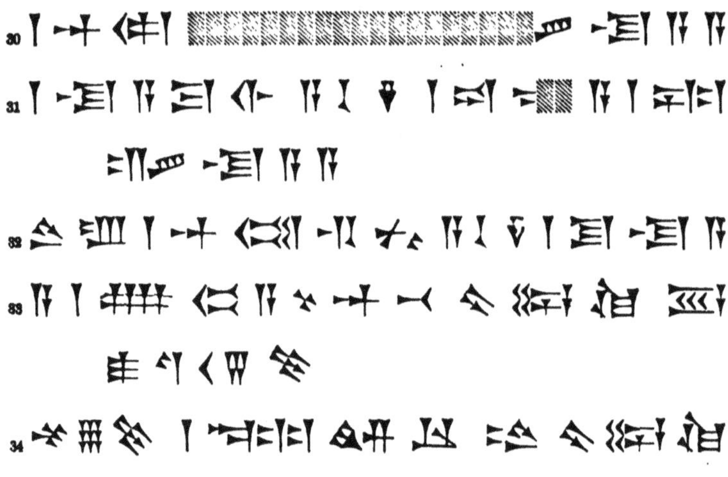

Tablet brown, with a decided pink tinge; 2¾ inches wide at the broadest, and 2⅝ inches long at the longest part. The three remaining edges are perfectly flat and smooth. According to my judgment more than half of the tablet below line 14 is broken off. In the middle of line 14 the tablet is 1¼ inches thick. This tablet has been published in autograph by Strassmaier in his texts No. 380, as well as by Pinches in *Hebraica* III, 13 ff. Peiser gives a transliteration and translation in Z. A. III, pp. 365–371. I would not have republished the tablet here, if it were not my intention to publish every cuniform text in the possession of the Metropolitan Museum of Art. This text contains 13 lines less than the one published by Pinches and Peiser, from whom the missing parts are supplied.

1 *Bil-ka-ṣir apal-šu ša Na-di-nu apal*
    Sag-gil-la-ai
2 *a-na Na-di-nu abi-šu apal-šu ša Ziri-ia*
    apal Sag-gil-la-ai
3 *iḳ-bi um-ma a-na bît mar-bâni-i taš-*
    pur-an-ni-ma Zu-un-na-a

4 *aš-ša-ti a-ḫu-uz-ma mâru u mârtu lâ*
    tul-du Bil-u-sat
5 *mâr-šu ša Zu-un-na-a mâr aššati-ia ša*
    la-pa-ni
6 *Ni-ḳu-du apal Nûr-Sin mu-ti-šu*
    maḫ-ru-u
7 *tu-li-du a-na mâru-u-tu lu-ul-ki-i-ma*

8 *lu-u mâru-u-a šu-u ina duppi mu- u-*
    ti-šu

9 *ti-ša-ab-ma išḳâtini u mîm-mu-ni*

10 *ma-la ba-šu-u ku-nu-uk-ma pa-ni-šu*
    šu-ud-gil-ma
11 *[l]u-u mâru ṣa-bit ḳâti-i-ni šu-u*
    Na-di-nu a-mat
12 *[Bil-ka-ṣ]ir mâr-šu iḳ-bu-šu lâ im-gur*
    Na-di-nu
13 *[a-na û-mu ru-ḳu-t]u man-ma ša-*
    nam-ma a-na lâ la-ki-t
14 *[išḳâti u nikasu-šu-nu]-tu dup-pi iš-*
    ṭur-ma

1 Belkasir, the son of Nadinu, the son
    of Saggillai,
2 to Nadinu, his father, the son of
    Ziria, the son of Saggillai,
3 spoke: "To the house of the adopted
    sons thou didst send me, and
    Zunnâ
4 I took to wife; but a son or a daugh-
    ter she bore (me) not: Belusat,
5 the son of Zunnâ, the son of my
    wife, whom unto
6 Nikudu, the son of Nûrsin, her former
    husband,
7 she bore, as my adopted son I will
    take:
8 verily he shall be my son. At (the
    writing of) the tablet concerning
    his adoption,
9 thou shalt be present. Our rights of
    income and our possessions,
10 as many as they may be, with seal
    write over to him.
11 Verily our adopted son shall he be.
    Nadinu, to the word (which)
12 Belkasir, his son had spoken, did
    not give his assent. (Then) Na-
    dinu,
13 that for eternal days no one else
    should seize
14 (his) rights of income and his ser-
    vices, wrote out a tablet.

(About 15 lines are missing. For the continuation of the text see Zeitschrift für Assyriologie III, pp. 366—368.)

30 *Nirgal .... [apal Sag-g]il-la-ai*
31 *La-a-ba-ši apal-šu ša Du-m[uḳ] apal*
    Sag-gil-la-ai
32 *(amilu) dupsar Marduk-bil-zir apal-šu*
    ša Su-la-a
33 *apal U-ṣur-a-mat-Bil Babilu(kᵢ) araḫ*
    Šabaṭu ûmu 15 kam

34 *šattu 9 kam Nabû-na'id šar Babili(ki)*

30 Nergal ...., the son of Saggillai;
31 Lâbashi, the son of Dumuk, the son
    of Saggillai;
32 the scribe Mardukbelzir, the son of
    Shulâ,
33 the son of Usuramatbel. Babylon,
    in the month Shabatu, on the 15th
    day,
34 in the 9th year of Nabonidus, King
    of Babylon.

Belkasir had married Zunnâ according to the wish of his father Nadinu. But Zunnâ proved to be barren. Belkasir, however, did not wish to depart this life without an heir, he therefore proposed the adoption of his step-son. To this Nadinu, for some reason, would not give his assent. Now Belkasir had every legal right to adopt Belusat, and he would undoubtedly have done so, had not his father made a will declaring that if Belkasir should have a natural and legal son, the latter should be the heir of his grandfather's fortune. If, however, this heir should not come to this world, then Belkasir should adopt his brother, and the latter would then become the heir of Nadinu's wealth. If Belkasir should be unwilling to adopt his brother (?), then he should adopt his sister. — The end of the tablet is unfortunately broken off, hence we can not learn the final result of all these hypotheses.

For a fuller explanation of this tablet see Z. A. III, 365—371.

NO. 55.

REVERSE.

This very fragmentary tablet, of which only part of the reverse is preserved, is of a light gray color, 1×1½ inches. The signs are very lightly, but finely, made. At least ten lines must be missing.

11 ....-*ši apal-šu* [*ša*]	11 . ..... shi, the son of ....,
12 [*apal*] .... *Ḳur-ban-ni-Marduk*	12 the son of ... .; Kurbannimarduk
13 *apal Irba-Nirgal Babilu(ki)*	13 the son of Irbanergal. Babylon,
14 *araḫ Tašritu ûmu 22 kam*	14 in the month Tashritu, on the 22nd day,

15 *šattu* 12 *kam Nabû-na'id* [*šar*] *Babili*(*ki*)	15 in the 12th year of Nabonidus, King of Babylon.

What this tablet purports to say, I am at a loss to tell. The only fact mentioned, besides the date, is that Kurbannimarduk is a witness.

NO. 56.

OBVERSE.

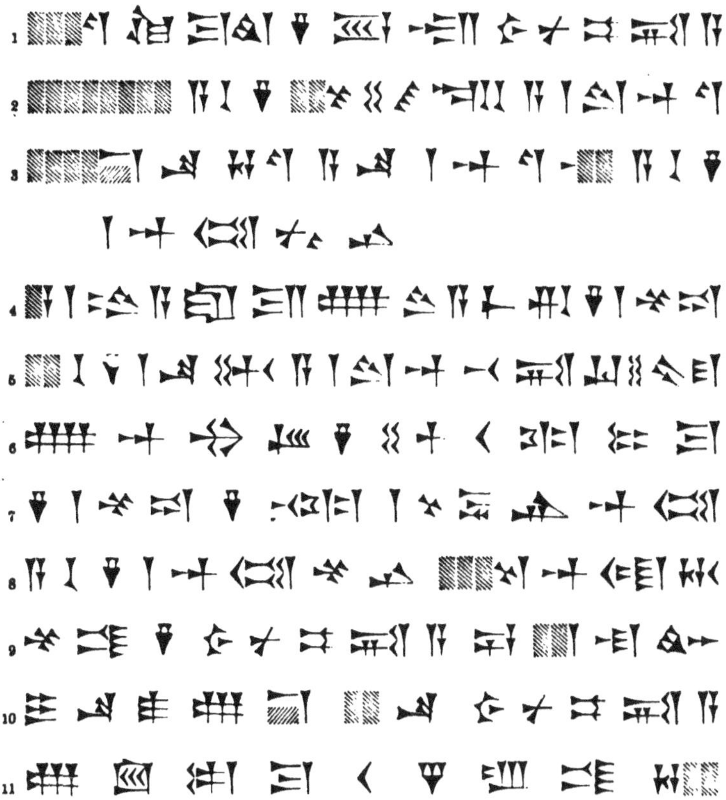

REVERSE.

Tablet brown; 1[illegible]×1[illegible] inches. The right upper corner of the obverse is broken off. And the surface of the obverse is as if pressed down with the finger before the tablet was baked. There are numerous cuts and strokes on the tablet, which were undoubtedly made by the careless scribe. Otherwise the signs are well made.

1 [*i-n*]*a ki-il ša araḫ Samna Nu-ub-ta-a*	1 At the end of the month Samna, Nûbtâ,
2 [*marat* ......] *apil-šu ša Mu-š-izib-Bîl apal Arad-Šamaš*	2 the daughter of ......; the son of Mushezibbel, the son of Aradshamash,
3 ...... *ma-na kaspi a-na Šamaš-iddin apal-šu ša Marduk-zir-ibni*	3 ...... mana of money to Shamashiddin, the son of Marduziribni,
4 *apal Šar-a-ra-zu-u* (*amilu*) *mâr šip-ri ša Šum-ukin*	4 the son of Shararazû, the messenger, for Shumukin,
5 [*apal*]-*šu ša Na-ṣir apal Arad-Bîl ta-nam-din-ma*	5 the son of Nasir, the son of Aradbel, will give.
6 *u-an-tim* (*mtš*) *ša ŠÍ.BAR u sulûpu*	6 The receipts for the grain and the dates
7 *ša Šum-ukin ša ina îli Ḳur-ban-ni-Marduk*	7 of Shumukin, which against Kurbannimarduk,
8 *apal-šu ša Marduk-šum-ibni* [*apal*] *Arad-Nirgal*	8 the son of Mardukshumibni, the son of Aradnergal,
9 *mu-tum ša Nu-ub-ta-a i-il-la-'*	9 the husband of Nûbtâ, are made out,
10 *i-na-aš-u-ma* [*a*]-*na Nu-ub-ta-a*	10 (the latter) will take, and to Nûbtâ
11 *u-bul-lam-ma u 4 ril-tum kas*[*pi*]	11 he will bring (them). And 4 certificates (?) for the money
12 *a-na Šamaš-iddin ta-nam-din-ma*	12 to Shamashiddin she will give.

13 *u-an-tim (-niš) a-na Nu-ub-ta-a*	13 The receipts to Nûbtâ
14 *i-nam-din (amilu) mu-kin Îṭir-Marduk apal-šu*	14 he will return. Witnesses: Etêrmarduk, the son
15 *ša Šum-ukin apal (ilu) Kib-na'id La-a-ba-ši*	15 of Shumukin, the son of Kibna'id; Lâbashi,
16 *apal-šu ša Nabû-idanin apal Mu-kal-lim Šapik-zir*	16 the son of Nabûidanin, the son of Mukallim; Shapikzir,
17 *(amîlu) dupsar apal-šu ša Îṭir-Bil apal Arad-Bil*	17 the scribe, the son of Etêrbel, the son of Aradbel.
18 *[a]lû ša Šum-ukin araḫ Samna ûmu 5 kam*	18 In the city of Shumukin, in the month Samna, on the 5th day,
19 *[šattu] 12 kam Nabû-na'id šar Babili(ki)*	19 in the 12th year of Nabonidus, King of Babylon.

Nûbtâ promised to pay a certain sum of money at the end of the month Marcheshwan (November) to Shamashiddin. The latter was in turn to pay it over to his master Shamashukin. This sum of money was due for grain and dates bought of Shamashukin. Now the bills had been made out in the name of Kurbannimarduk, the husband of Nûbtâ. He naturally turned them over to his wife, who had contracted the debt. Nûbtâ then issued four bonds which she gave to Shamashiddin, in order to insure her payment of the money. As soon as she had paid the proper amount, these certificates or bonds would naturally be returned to her, as lines 13 and 14 state. The debt had about 25 days to run, and therefore, probably, no interest was to be paid.

NO. 57.

OBVERSE.

REVERSE.

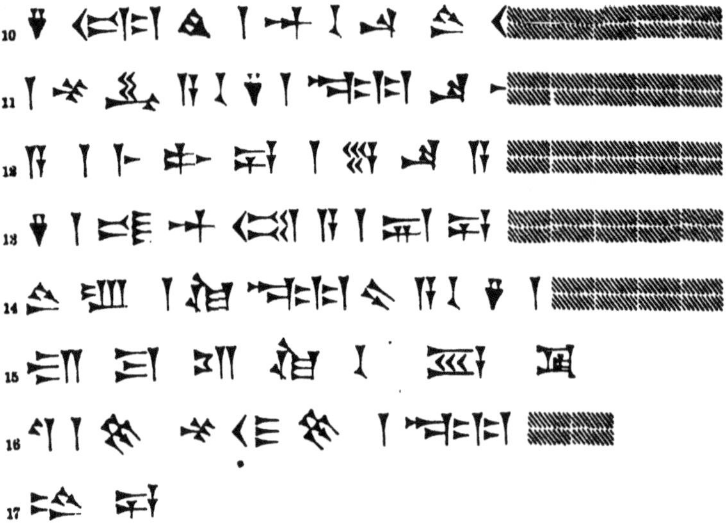

Tablet light gray; at the longest side 1⅞, and at the broadest 1¼ inches. The right edge, with part of the tablet, is totally destroyed. The signs are very blurred and difficult to decipher. There are no wedges on the left and the upper edges.

1 66 *gur suluppu zak̦-pi ša* ....
2 *apal-šu ša Balaṭu apal Î-sag-gil-ai* [*ina ili*]
3 *Bîl-iṭir-napšâti Marduk-*......[*u*]
4 *Nabû-zir-kaṣir ina araḫ Tašritu š*[*im*]
5 *gam-ru-tu ina ḫa-ṣa-ri i*[*t-ti*] ...... [*gur*]
6 *tu-ḫal-la lib-bi kas-pa* (?) ......
7 *bil-tum ša ḫu-ṣa-bi* ......
8 *i-nam-din-nu išti-in p*[*u-ut*]

1 66 gur dates, the planting, which....,
2 the son of Balatu, the son of Esaggillai, (is to receive of)
3 Beletérnapshâti, Marduk ......, and
4 Nabûzirkasir. In the month Tashritu, at the
5 full price, during the harvesting, together with ...... gur of
6 unripe dates, for money (?) ......
7 talents of date ......
8 they will give. One receipt

9 *[i]-na-šu u i-lat ra-[šu-tu]*	9 he will bring. And in addition there is the balance
10 *ša ili Marduk-kaṣir (amilu)* ...... *[ša]*	10 in favor of Mardukkasir, the ......, (which)
11 *Šum-uṣur apla-šu ša Nabû-na-[ṣir]*	11 Shumusur, the son of Nabûnasir,
12 *apal Mi-pi-i Iddin-na-apla [apal-šu]*	12 the son Mepê, (and) Iddinnapla, the son
13 *ša Îrîš-Bil apal Bil-i-*	13 of Ereshbel, the son of Bite ......, (will give).
14 *(amilu) dupsar Itti-Nabû-balaṭu apal-šu ša*	14 Scribe: Ittinabûbalatu, the son of ....
15 *alû Ma-mil-ki-šu araḫ Ululu*	15 In the city Mamilkishu, in the month Ululu,
16 *ûmu 1 kam šattu 13 kam Nabû-[na'id]*	16 on the 1st day, in the 13th year of Nabonidus,
17 *šar Babili*	17 King of Babylon

Beletêrnapshâti, Marduk..... , and Nabûzirkasir, who were farmers or gardeners, promise to sell 66 gur of dates to the son of Balatu. They will also sell him unripe dates, and something else connected with the date-palm (line 7), at a specified price. Now this son of Balatu seems to have purchased the account of Mardukkasir, to whom some dates were due from Shumusur and Iddinnapla. The last named two men must have stood in some intimate relation with the three mentioned in lines 3 and 4, otherwise they would not have been mentioned on this tablet and in this connection.

NO. 58.

OBVERSE.

About two lines on the obverse, and two on the reverse are broken off.

REVERSE.

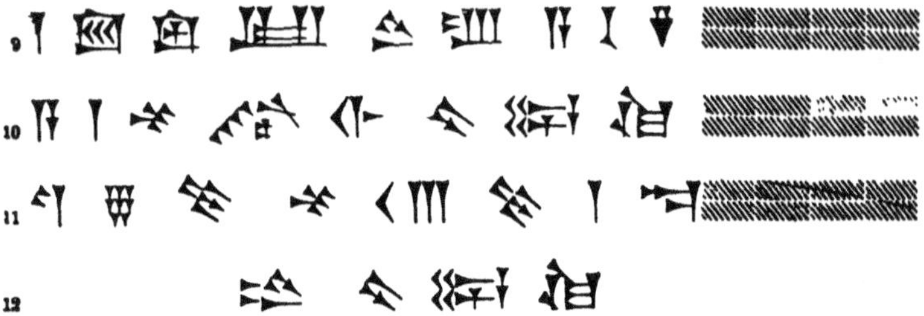

Tablet gray; 1⅛×1⅛ inches. A fragment. The signs are crude. The right side and about 4 lines upon the lower edge, are broken off. The left and upper edges are not written upon.

1 5 *šiḳlu bit-ḳa kaspi ša*	1 5 coined shekels of money, which ....,
2 *marat-su ša Šapik-zir ina ili*	2 the daughter of Shapikzir is to receive from ....,
3 *apal-šu ša Ba-la-ṭu apal Mar-[duk]*	3 the son of Balatu, the son of Marduk ......,
4 *u Na-'-it-tum [marat-su ša]*	4 and Na'ittum, (the daughter of) ....

About four lines are broken off.

9 *Bul-lu-ṭu (amilu) dupsar apal-šu ša*	9 Bullutu, the scribe, the son of ......,
10 *apal Mu-lul-lim Babilu(ki) [araḫ]*	10 the son of Mulullim. Babylon, in the month ......,
11 *ûmu 8 kam šattu 13 kam Na[bû-na'id]*	11 on the 8th day, in the 13th year of Nabonidus,
12 *šar Babili(ki)*	12 King of Babylon.

This tablet merely records the small debt of five shekels, which the son of Balatu and Na'ittum were to pay to the daughter of Shapikzir. Whether interest was to be paid or not, we can not tell, as that interesting fact may have been contained in the four lost lines.

NO. 59.

OBVERSE.

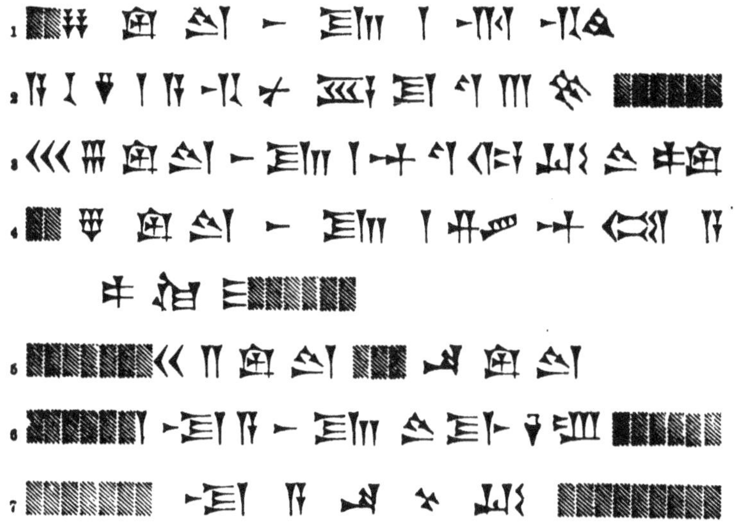

REVERSE.

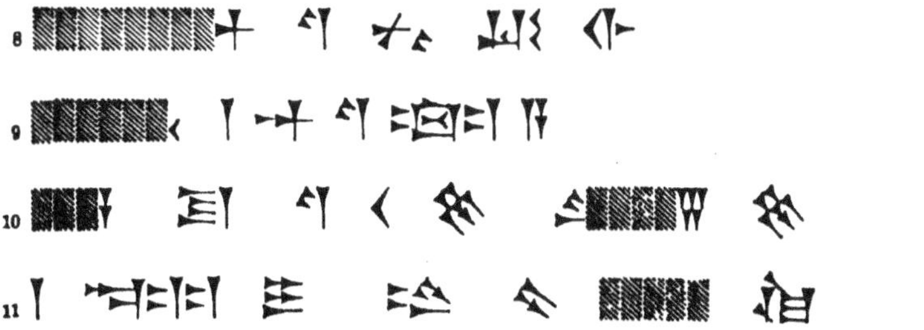

Tablet 1⅛×2⅜ inches. In very bad condition. The corners, excepting the upper right hand one of the obverse, are broken off. There is a large hole in line 5. The last two lines are badly marred. The space seems to indicate the 15th year.

1 + 6 *LU.NITA ina kâtâ Ri-mut*	1 + 6 sheep are to be received from Rimut,
2 [*apal*]-*šu ša A-ḫu-nu araḫ Dûzu ûmu* 3 *kam*	2 the son of Ahunu, in the month Dûzu, on the 3rd day;

3 36 *LU.NITA ina ḳâtâ Šamaš-mudammi-iḳ (amîlu) ri'u*	3 36 sheep from Shamashmudammik, the shepherd;
4 + 7 *LU.NITA ina ḳâtâ Musallim-Marduk apal pa-ki-r[a-nu]*	4 +7 sheep from Musallimmarduk, the son of the overseer;
5 + 22 *LU.NITA i-na LU.NITA*	5 + 22 sheep, as .... sheep,
6 ...... *-la-a ina ḳâtâ (amîlu) rab ša bangi*	6 from the chief of the priests,
7 ...... *lâ a-na šad-ik*	7 ...... not for slaughter ......
8 [*(amîlu) dupsar*] *Šamaš-zir-gal-lim*	8 Scribe: Shamashzirgallim,
9 [*apal-šu ša*] *Šamaš-dûr-a*	9 the son of Shamashdûra.
10 [*ara*]*ḫ Dûzu ûmu 10 kam šattu 15(?) kam*	10 In the month Dûzu, on the 10th day, in the 15th year of
11 *Nabû-na'id šar Babili(ki)*	11 Nabonidus, King of Babylon.

This tablet gives a list of the sheep and of those that offered them, probably in the temple at Sippara.

NO. 60.

OBVERSE.

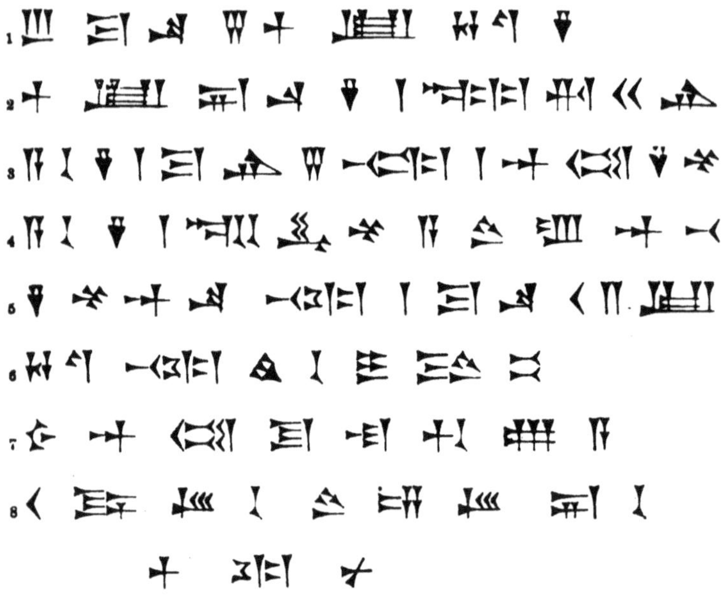

REVERSE.

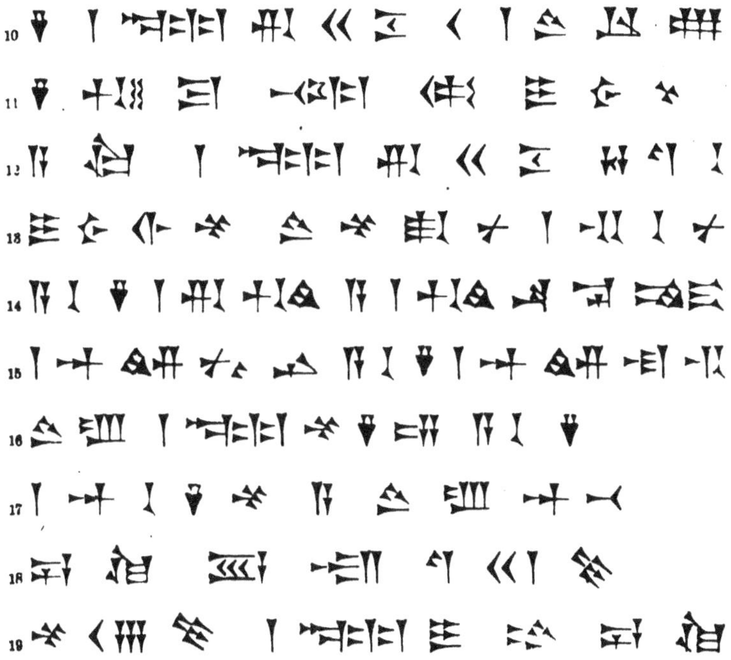

Tablet dark brown shading to black; $1\frac{5}{8} \times 1\frac{7}{8}$ inches. The tablet has been very roughly used, judging by the blurred appearance of the signs. The left edge contains no writing, the right edge but a few signs of prolonged lines. The edges and corners are perfect; the whole tablet is preserved.

1 *⅓ ma-na 5½ šiḳlu kaspi ša*	1 ⅓ mana 5½ shekels of money, which
2 *ina 1 šiḳlu bit-ḳa ša Nabû-ri-man-ni*	2 is divided into single shekels, which Nabûrimanni.
3 *apal-šu ša Ba-ni-ia ina ili Marduk-šakin-šum*	3 the son of Bania, is to receive from Mardukshakinshum,
4 *apal-šu ša Bil-uṣur-šum apal (amilu) šangu Bil*	4 the son of Belusurshum, the son of the priest of Bel;
5 *ša šatti ina ili 1 ma-na 12 šiḳlu*	5 every year, upon one mana, twelve shekels of
6 *kaspi ina ili-šu i-rab-bi*	6 money shall increase against him.
7 *Marduk-šu-la-ḫu-u-a*	7 Mardukshulahûa
8 *u mâri-šu (amilu) niši bîti-šu*	8 and her sons, the slaves of his house,
9 *maš-ka-nu*	9 are the security
10 *ša Nabû-ri-man-ni u (amilu) rašu-u*	10 of Nabûrimanni. And a creditor,

11 *ša-nam-ma ina ili ul i-šal-laṭ*	11 whoever he be, over (the slaves) shall have no say
12 *a-di Nabû-ri-man-ni kaspa-šu*	12 until Nabûrimanni his money
13 *i-šal-lim-mu (amilu) mu-kin-nu Bil-šu-nu*	13 shall have received. Witnesses: Belshunu,
14 *apal-šu ša Ri-mut apal Mut-na-si-bii*	14 the son of Rimut, the son of Mutnasibil;
15 *Rammânu-zir-ibni apal-šu ša Rammânu-la-bak*	15 Rammânziribni, the son of Rammânlabak.
16 *(amilu) dupsar Nabû-šum-iškun-un apal-šu ša*	16 Scribe: Nabushumishkun, the son of
17 *Marduk-šakin-šum apal (amilu) šangu Bil*	17 Mardukshakinshun, the son of the priest of Bel.
18 *Babilu(ki) araḫ Samna ûmu 21 kam*	18 Babylon, in the month Samna, on the 21st day,
19 *šattu 16 kam Nabû-na'id šar Babili(ki)*	19 in the 16th year of Nabonidus, King of Babylon.

Mardukshakinshum loaned ⅓ mana 5⅓ shekels of money from Nabûrimanni. This money had been paid out in single shekels, therefore Mardukshakinshum received 25⅓ pieces of coin. Now this money is to bear interest, the rate of interest to be 12 shekels on 60 for every year, hence 20 per cent. Until the loan is repaid, the female slave of Mardukshakinshum, together with her sons, are to be security. These slaves, it is especially stipulated, can not be given as security to another creditor of their master, nor can they be disposed of by the latter, until Nabûrimanni's claim has been settled.

NO. 61.

OBVERSE.

REVERSE.

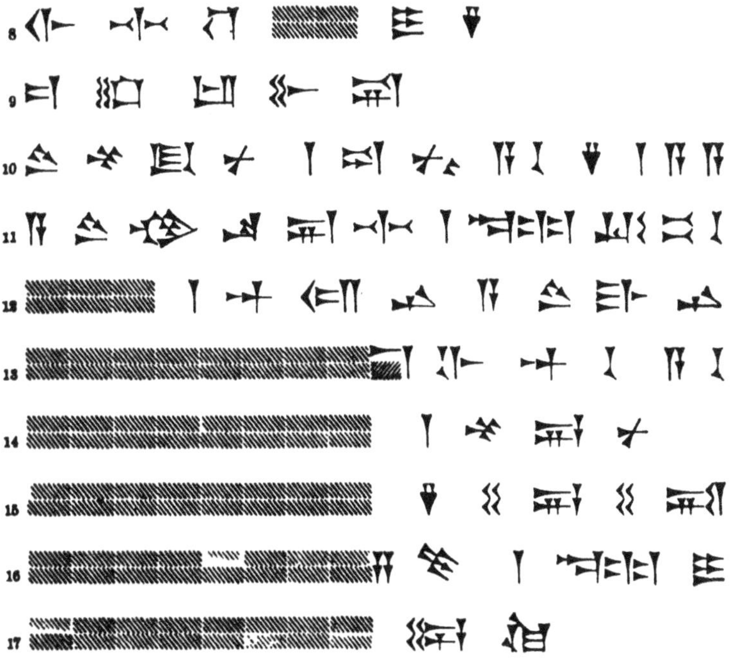

Tablet brown, with numerous black spots; 1¼×1¾ inches. The left upper corner of the obverse is destroyed, thus breaking off the beginning of the last few lines of the reverse. The left edge is not written upon.

1 ...... [*gur*] *ŠÍ.BAR ša Šum-ukin*	1 ...... gur of grain which Shumukin,
2 [*apal-šu ša*] ......*na-ṣir apal Arad-Bil*	2 the son of ......nasir, the son of Aradbel,
3 *ina íli Marduk-šum-iddin apal-šu ša*	3 is to receive of Mardukshumiddin, the son of
4 *Arad-Bil apal Arad-Bil*	4 Aradbel, the son of Aradbel.
5 *ina araḫ Airu ina ḳaḳḳadi-šu* 14 *gur*	5 In the month Airu, in his sum total, 14 gur (of grain)
6 *id-dup-tum ina bâbu Ka-lak-ku*	6 as ......, in the gate Kalakku,
7 *i-nam-din í-lat u-an-tim*	7 he will give. In addition a receipt
8 *u šib ti tu* [*í-pi*]-*i-ša*	8 and a bond (?) were given (that)
9 (*iṣu*) *kirû ip-pu-uš*	9 he will make a park.
10 (*amílu*) *mu-kin-nu Ukin-zir apal-šu ša*	10 Witnesses: Ukinzir, the son of Ai,

11 *apal (amilu) ṭûbtu na-bil-ti Nabû-iḳ-bi-šu*	11 the son of the .. .. man; Nabu-ikbishu,
12 [*apal-šu ša*] *Nirgal-ibni apal (amîlu) rab bâni*	12 the son of Nergalibni, the son of the chief carpenter;
13 ......*tuk-Marduk apal-šu*	13 ....tukmarduk, the son
14 [*ša*] ...... [*apal*] *Šum-idan-nu*	14 of ...., the son of Shumidannu;
15 ...... *ša ši dan ši ta*	15 ....
16 ...... [*šattu*] + 4 *kam Nabû-na'id*	16 In the month ......, on the .... day, in the +4th year of Nabonidus,
17 [*šar*] *Babili(ki)*	17 King of Babylon.

Shumukin is to receive from Mardukshumiddin a certain quantity of grain. In the month Airu (May) the latter promises to give 14 measures in the gate Kalakku (see Peiser, B. V. VI 5). In addition to this, lines 7 - 9 seem to say, he is to make a park for Shumukin. The labor connected with this is probably to count the same as the delivery of several measures of grain. Lines 8 and 15 are too blurred to be properly deciphered.

NO. 62.

OBVERSE.

About four lines on the obverse, and four on the reverse are broken off.

REVERSE.

Tablet a fragment of dark gray color with dark olive spots; ⅞×1⅛ inches. The right upper side is perfect; the left side is effaced, and the lower portion is totally destroyed. The upper and right edges contained no writing. About 8 lines are missing.

1 ...... *gur ŠI.BAR* 2 *pi a-ba-aḫ ši-in-nu*	1 ...... gur of grain, 2 pi of ....
2 ...... *bit-li-i-ma* 20 ...... *ḳa-ai tu-mi-mi*	2 ...... vessels of spices, 20 ....
3 ...... *ba-u-i ša La-ba-[a-š]i*	3 .... of Labâshi,
4 [*apal-šu ša Ba-la-ṭu apal Šag-gil-la-ai*	4 the son of Balatu, the son of Saggillai.

About 8 lines are missing.

13 ....*-im araḫ Airu ûmu* 1 *kam*	13 ...., in the month Airu, on the first day,
14 [*šattu*] ...... *kam* [*Nabû*]*-na'id šar*	14 in the ..th year of Nabonidus, King
15 *Babili(ki)*	15 of Babylon.

This exceedingly fragmentary tablet gives a list of goods belonging to Labâshi. Whether he is to receive them from somebody else, or to give them, or whether this is merely a list or inventory, the fragmentary state of the tablet will not allow us to determine.

NO. 63.

OBVERSE.

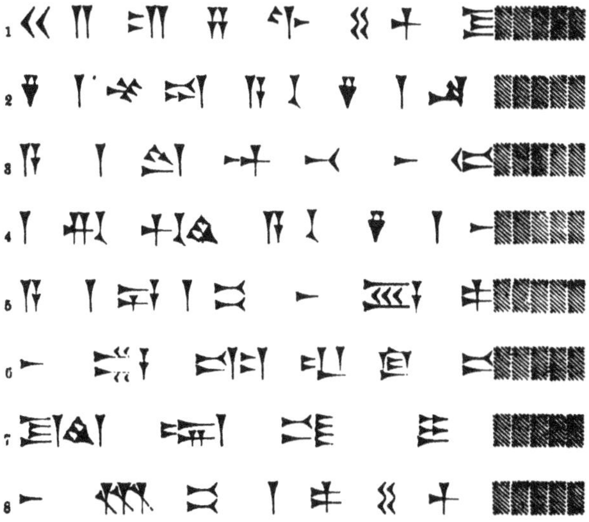

REVERSE.

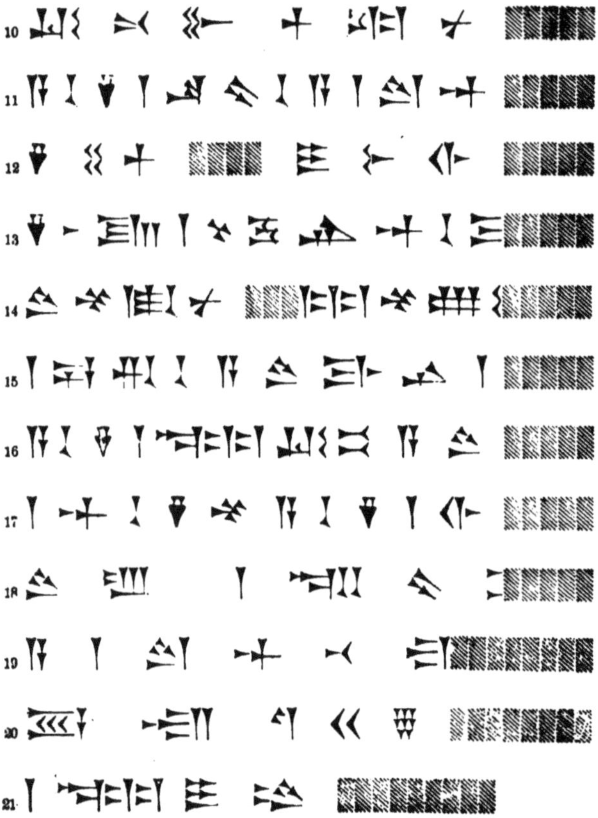

Tablet dark gray; $1\frac{3}{8}\times1\frac{3}{8}$ inches. A fragment. The tablet is much damaged. The right side is completely effaced.

1 22 *gur* 4 *pi* *ŠÍ.BAR ša-[ul-la(?)]*
2 *ša Šum-ukin apal-šu ša Na-* .....
3 *apal Arad-Bêl ina i[li]*
4 *Ri-mut apal-šu ša* ......
5 *apal Ê-gi-bi ina araḫ Airu [ša šatta*
...... *kam]*

1 22 gur 4 pi of grain, over and above
2 which Shumukin, the son of Na....,
3 the son of Aradbel, is to receive from
4 Rimut, the son of ....,
5 the son of Egibi. In the month
Airu, of the ..th year,

6 *ina bâbi Ka-lak-ku ḳa[ḳḳadi-šu]*	6 in the gate Kalakku, his sum total,
7 *id-dup-tum i-[nam-din]*	7 namely the ......, he will give
8 *ina lib-bi* 1 *pi ŠÍ.BAR*	8 Thereof 1 pi grain, and .... (measures of)
9 *ŠÍ.ZIR-šu zaḳ-[pi]*	9 his seed field, planted with ....
10 *iḳ-ḳa-bu maš-ka-nu*	10 are called the security. ....
11 *apal-šu ša Na-din-šu apal Arad-(ilu)*	11 the son of Nadishu, the son of Arad ......, (is witness that the money)
12 *ša ŠÍ.BAR* ...... *i-pu-ši*	12 for the grain of ...... was paid ....
13 *ša ina ḳâtâ Ḳur-ban-ni-Marduk* [*mâr*]	13 which was received from Kurbannimarduk, (the son of) ......
14 (*amilu*) *mu-kin-nu* [*Na*]*bû-šum-u-ṣ[ur apal-šu ša]*	14 Witnesses: Nabûshumusur, the son of
15 *Í-ri-šu apal* (*amilu*) *rab bâni*	15 Erishu, the son of the chief carpenter; ......
16 *apal-šu ša Nabû-iḳ-bi apal* (*amilu*)....	16 the son of Nabûikbi, the son of the ......;
17 *Marduk-šakin-šum apal-šu ša Ši*.	17 Mardukshakinshum, the son of Shi........
18 (*amilu*) *dupsar Bíl-uballi-i[ṭ]*	18 Scribe, Beluballit,
19 *apal Arad-Bíl alû*	19 the son of Aradbel. In the city ....
20 *araḫ Samna ûmu* 28 [*kam šattu*]...... [*kam*]	20 in the month Samna, on the 28th day, in the ..th year of
21 *Nabû-na'id šar* [*Babili(ki)*]	21 Nabonidus, King of Babylon.

Shumukin is to receive 22 gur 4 pi of grain from Rimut. The latter promises to deliver it in the month Airu of the ..th year, in the gate Kalakku (see Peiser, B. V. VI 5). But Rimut has evidently already received his pay. He is therefore required to offer some security. This he offers in the shape of grain and cultivated land. The son of Nadinshu had seen Rimut receive his pay from the hands of Kurbannimarduk, hence Rimut can not retreat from his agreement.

NO. 64.

OBVERSE.

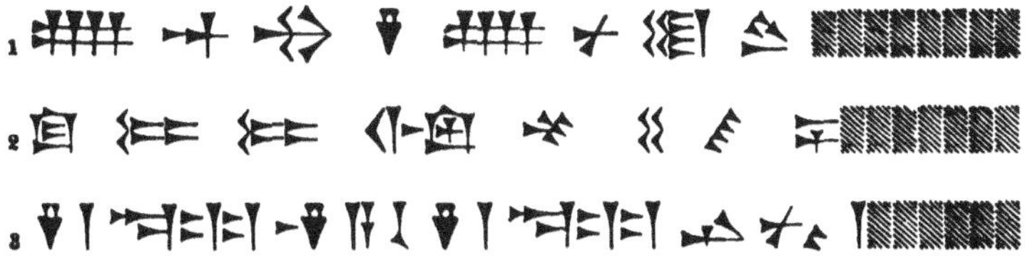

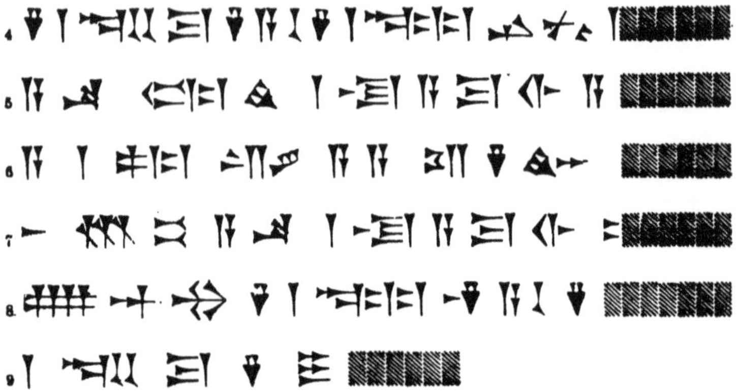

About one line on the obverse, and two on the reverse are broken off.

REVERSE.

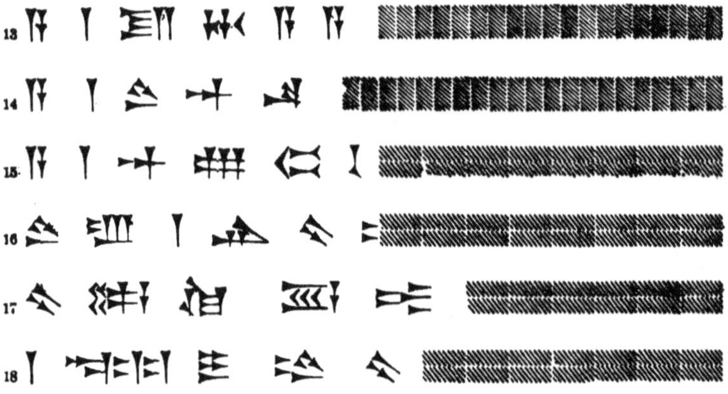

Tablet dark gray shading to black; $1\frac{3}{4}\times2\frac{1}{4}$ inches at the broadest and longest parts. The right and lower edges are destroyed. The right side of the reverse is totally effaced. The signs are very plainly made.

1 *u-an-tim ša u-nu-tu (amîlu)* ......

2 *ṣubatu ušḫubu u mu-ši-zib* ......

1 The receipt for the utensils of the ...... man,

2 (for) ...... garments and loans (?) ....

3 *ša Nabû-iṭir apal-šu ša Nabû-ibni-zir*
   a[pal] . . . .[u]

4 *ša Bil-iḳi-ša apal-šu ša 'Nabû-ibni-zir*
   a[pal] . . . . . .

5 *a-na ili La-a-ba-ši apal-[šu ša]* . . . . . .

6 *apal Sa-gil-ai iš-ša-'*

7 *ina lib-bi a-na La-a-ba-ši* . . . . .

8 *u-an-tim ša Nabû-iṭir apal-šu ša*
   [*Nabû-ibni-zir*]

9 *Bil-iḳi-ša i-[nam-din]*

---

3 that belonged to Nabûetêr, the son of
   Nabûibnizir, the sou of . . . .,
   (and)

4 that belonged to Belikisha, the son
   of Nabûibnizir, the son of . . . . . .,

5 to the account of Lâbashi, the son
   of . . . . . .,

6 the son of Saggillai, is made out.

7 Thereafter to Lâbashi, ...,

8 the receipt of Nabûetêr, the son of
   Nabûibnizir,

9 Belikisha will give.

Lines 10, 11 and 12 are effaced.

13 *apal Su-ḫa-ai* . . . . . .

14 *apal amîlu (ilu) Na-[na-a]* . . . . . .

15 *apal Ilu-u-ṣur-šu* . . . .

16 (*amîlu*) *dupsar Ni-din-tu[m apal-šu*
   ša] . . . . . .

17 *Babilu(ki) araḫ Kisilimu [ûmu]* . . . . . .
   [*kam šattu*] . . . . [*kam*]

18 *Nabû-na'id šar Ba[bili(ki)]*

---

13 the son of Suhai; . . . . . .

14 the son of the priest of Nanâ;

15 the son of Ilusurshu; . . . . . .

16 Scribe: Nidintum, the son of . . . . . .

17 Babylon, in the month Kisilimu, on
   the . . .th day, in the . .th year of

18 Nabonidus, King of Babylon.

Nabûetêr and Belikisha, two brothers, sold a certain amount of implements, clothes, and other things. The bill was to be paid by Lâbashi. Nabûetêr had evidently commissioned his brother Belikisha to look after his interests. Therefore Lâbashi was to pay the sum of money due the two brothers of Belikisha, and the latter was to give the former his receipt together with that of his brother. The remainder of the tablet, from line 10 on contained only the names of the witnesses and the date.

NO. 65.

OBVERSE.

REVERSE.

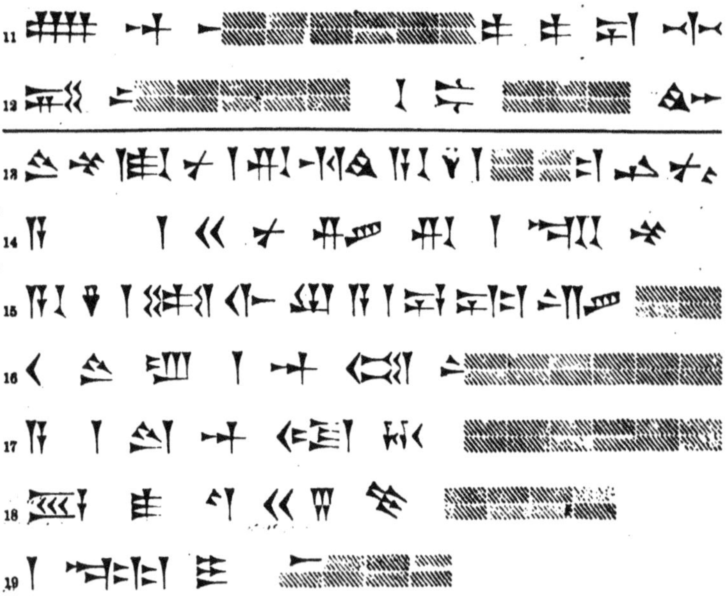

Tablet light gray; 1¼×2 inches. The signs are blurred, and a considerable portion of the surface of the tablet has crumbled off. The right upper corner, extending half the length and breadth of the tablet, is broken off. A bad break is also found on the lower edge. The tablet is very difficult to decipher.

1 18 *gur ŠÍ.BAR* [*ša* (*ilu*) *Daînu-šum-iddin*]	1 18 gur of grain, which Dainushumiddin,
2 *apal-šu ša Ṣil-la-a* [*apal*] ...... [*ina ili*]	2 the son of Sillâ, the son of ......, is to receive from
3 *Nabû-apal-iddin apal-šu ša Marduk-irba apal*	3 Nabûapaliddin, the son of Marduk-irba, the son of ......
4 *ina araḫ Dûzu ḳaḳḳadu-šu i-nam-din* 26 *gur*	4 In the month Dûzu he will give his amount. 18 gur
5 *ša pir'u ma-tum ša araḫ Dûzu pân Bêlit-aḫrâtu niḳ*[*u*]	5 of seed-land, during the month Dûzu, are for the goddess Belit-ahrâtu, the sacrifice
6 *ša* (*ilu*) *Daînu-šum-iddin ši i Ri-kiš-šak-la-*......	6 of Dainushumiddin is it. Rikish-shakla......,
7 *gal-la-šu maš-ka-nu ša* (*ilu*) *Daînu-šum-iddin*	7 his slave, is the security of Dainu-shumiddin.
8 (*amilu*) *rašu-u ša-nam-ma* (*ina*) *ili ul i-šal-laṭ*	8 Another creditor shall have no say over him.
9 *pap-pa-su a*[*-na ma*]*š-šar-tum ša araḫ Ṭibitu*	9 (His) sustenance till the end of the month Tebitu
10 *Nabû-apal-iddin* [*a-na*] (*ilu*) *Daînu-šum-iddin i-ṭir*	10 Nabûapaliddin will pay to Dainu-shumiddin.
11 *u-an-t*[*im* (*miš*)] .... *pa*(?) *i ti*	11 The receipts for ....
12 *gab-bi* .... *šu-ub-*[*la-a*]-'	12 all (of them) ......, he will cause to be brought.
13 (*amilu*) *mu-kin-nu Ri-mut apal-šu ša Nabû-ibni-zir*	13 Witnesses: Rimut, the son of Nabû-ibnizir,
14 *apal Man-nu-gi-ri Bêl iddin*	14 the son of Mannugiri; Beliddin,
15 *apal-šu ša Li-ši-ru apal Î-sag-gil-*[*ia-ai*]	15 the son of Lishiru, the son of Esag-gillai;
16 *u* (*amilu*) *dupsar Marduk-šum* ..... [*apal-šu ša*]	16 and the scribe Mardukshum......; the son of ......,
17 *apal Arad-Nirgal* [*Babilu*(*ki*)]	17 the son of Aradnergal. Babylon (?),
18 *araḫ Šabaṭu ûmu* 25 *kam* [*šattu*] .... [*kam*]	18 in the month Shabatu, on the 25th day, in the ..th year of
19 *Nabu-na'id š*[*ar Babili*(*ki*)]	19 Nabonidus, King of Babylon.

Dainushumiddin is to receive from Nabûapaliddin 18 gur of grain. The latter promises to deliver them in the month Dûzu (July). These 18 gur have already been vowed to the goddess Belit-ahrâtu by Dainushumiddin, and the latter has also promised to have them delivered in the same month. Consequently he must be severe in demanding the grain at the proper time. He, therefore, takes Rikishshakla ...., the slave of Nabûapaliddin as security, and by means of line 8, denies the right of any other creditor of Nabûapaliddin to have any say over the slave. He even demands sustenance for the latter, for five months beyond the time, when the payment of the grain has become due. Lines 11 and 12 seem to imply that after all requirements have been satisfied, Daiunshumiddin will cause all the necessary receipts to be handed over to his debtor Nabûapaliddin.

NOTES.

No. 1. Line 1. *ina ili ina pân* is a double expression of one and the same idea, as *ina ili* and *ina pân* are used interchangeably in the contract tablets.

Lines 3, 5. *ṣíni* Brünnow C. L. 10253.

Line 6. *ta-lit-tu* is propably a *t* formation of the stem *alâdu*, Heb. ילד meaning "to beget"; hence, tentatively, "the young."

Line 10. The sign *ni* is written on the tablet by mistake for *kak*.

Line 12. *Nippuru*. See Brünnow C. L. 2977.

No. 2. Line 1. ½ *šiḳlu* 6 *šiḳlu* written instead of 6½ *šiḳlu*.

Line 7. According to Strassmaier, Cambyses Nos. 195, 226, 286, *Bil-ki-šir* is the son of *Šu-la-a*, of the family of Egibi. In this tablet, however, only the family names are given.

Line 9. *ûmu* is omitted by the scribe, and *šattu* 12 *kam* is repeated by mistake in the next line.

Line 10. In tablets Nos. 2 and 3 of this part a final phonetic syllable *na* is added to Shamashshumukin's (Saosduchinos) name. In No. 4, however, it is omitted.

No. 3. Lines 1, 12. *Šu-la-a*. To be read thus though *Šu-ba-a* is written.

Line 8. Notice the curious form of *maḫ*.

Line 14.  for 

No. 4. Line 1. *ni-is-ḫu*. See Tallqvist p. 105, and Peiser, K. A. II [98].

Line 5. *u-tir*. From *utru*. See Strass. Neb. 261 [6]; also Part I of this book, where it occurs in the form *u-tur* 18 [6] 15 [5].

No. 5. Lines 3, 5, 6. (*ilu*) *Ṣa-bit-bit*. Strassmaier reads (*ilu*) *Zamame*.

Lines 7, 8. The last sign is the sign of repetition, and means that *TU.BIT* (*ilu*) *Ṣa-bit-bit* is to be repeated.

Line 11. (*amilu*) *PI.IR.MÍŠ*, if read syllabically (*amîlu*) *pi-ir* (*mîš*), may mean "seedsmen," though there is no reason why the plural should have been used.

No. 61. Line 5. Usually the tens precede the units, but the reverse is the case here.

No. 62. Line 1. *ši-in-nu* occurs also in Strass. Nabn. 558, 10.

No. 64. Line 1. *u-nu-tu* "utensils." Consult A. & W. Sanh. I, 28.

Line 2. *ušhubu*, according to Brünnow C. L. 11188.

Line 14. (*amílu*) (*ilu*) *Na*-[*na-a*]. *šangu* is omitted. This a frequent omission on the contract tablets.

No. 65. Line 5. *pir'u ma-tum* is evidently another phrase for *ŠĪ.ZIR* translated by Peiser "seed (field)." Here *pir'u* is equivalent to *ŠĪ.BAR* of line 1, and *ma-tum* is added to complete the phrase.

Bilit-aḫrâtu (Brünnow C. L. 11523) "Belit of the Future," "Belit, Goddess of Futurity."

Line 14. *-šu ša* seems to be erased in this line on the tablet, as is indicated by the space.

www.ingramcontent.com/pod-product-compliance
Lightning Source LLC
Chambersburg PA
CBHW050014090426
42734CB00020B/3261
* 9 7 8 1 6 3 1 8 2 8 3 4 8 *